KITEBOARDING
Vision

Imagination gives you the picture.
Vision gives you the impulse to make the picture your own.

Robert Collier

www.ikorg.com

Note: Despite some of the pictures included on this book, IKO strongly recommends kiteboarding with a kite leash and a helmet.

Author: *Eric Beaudonnat*

Eric has been kiteboarding since 1997 and is a professional sports instructor since 1991. Co founder of the IKO (International Kiteboarding Organization) his various trips in different parts of the world to teach kiteboarders and train kiteboard instructors has brought him a global vision of the sport and thorough knowledge, which he shares with us in this book.

PHOTO CREDIT

Airush	(Erik Ader)
Cabrinha	(Stephen Whitesell)
Flexifoil	(John Carter)
Flysurfer.de	
F-one	(Manu Morel)
G.W.A.	(Boris Pilipenko)
IKO	(Eric Beaudonnat)
Litewave	(Stephen Whitesell, Jeff Pfeffer)
Peter Lynn	
Sami Jukkara	
Slingshot	(John Bilderback)
Takoon	(Hugo Ljunberg, Manu Morel)
Tarmo Laine	
Bruno Legaignoux	

ACKNOWLEDGEMENTS

I would like to thank the people who have participated, one way or the other, in this book: Gaël, Xavier, Susie, Sophie, Fred, Sandrine, William, Niklas, Jonathan, Hans, and Jon (Dominican Republic), Jerry and Beto (Brasil), Mike and Milo (South Africa), Vesku (Finland), Hamid (Kuwait), Alejandro (Argentina), Jimmy Lewis (Hawaii), and Murray (Venezuela).

I would also like to thank Yves Belliard, who gave me the opportunity to start kiteboarding, Manu Bertin, who taught me the basis, and Bruno Legaignoux for teaching me the technical aspects of the sport.

Practical tools

Insert	Plastic or metal part in which the footstrap fastening nails are introduced
Jibe	Change of direction on a directional board while changing the feet positioning
Leader lines	The lines that connect the bar to the flying lines. The leader lines are strengthened at their connection point to the bar to avoid injury
Leading edge	Front of the kite where the air flows through first, the leading edge is larger than the trailing edge
Leash	Strap that connects the rider to the board or to a safety system on the kite
Lift	Power of the kite that pulls towards the top or during jumps
Lift (2)	Back curve of the board's profile
Lower skin (intrados)	Internal surface of a kite
Luff up	Going from one direction to the next closer to the wind
Mutant	Small directional board that has one or more fins at the front
Off the lip	Making a turn on the top (crest) of a wave
Passive security	That reduces the consequences of an accident. An automatic safety, a protection, a physical condition
Port	Left
Quick release	Safety system that releases the bar or one of the lines
Rail	The sides of a board
Regular	Person who uses his left foot as front foot
Rigging	Setting up the equipment
Rocker	Curve of the board when you look at the profile from the nose to the tail
Sailing points	Sailing direction according to the wind (upwind, beam-reach, broad-reach...)
Scoop	Curve of the board when you look at the front part of the profile
Shape	The design of a board
Shaper	Person who designs and builds boards
Spot	Place where people go kiteboarding
Starboard	Right
Strut	Part that keeps the profile of the kite. Inflatable or in fibre.
Tantrum	Trick: jump with a front rotation, with the back turned in the opposite riding direction
The top	Position of the kite right above the head of the pilot, at the zenith of the wind window (neutral)
Tip	Tip of the kite
Toe stance	Position where the rider edges on his toes
Top skin (extrados)	External surface of a kite
Trailing edge	Opposite to the leading edge, back of the kite
Transition	Aerial move resulting in a change of direction
Twin tip	Symmetric board that has fins at the front and the back
Upwind	What we see when we look towards the wind, with the wind blowing in front of us
Upwind riding	Going upwind
Vortex	Whirlwind at the tip of the kite, created when the wind under and over the kite meet

KITEBOARDER'S GLOSSARY

Active security	It's how to avoid an accident. An action, a safety system, an analysis, a reflex, the choice of a safe spot
Bear away	Changing direction with a bigger angle according to the wind. To achieve that, we put pressure on the toes
Angle of attack	Angle between the wind and the cord of the kite
Apparent wind	The apparent wind is the sum of the "true wind" and the wind generated by the motion of the kiteboarder, or the wind you feel when you move
Aspect ratio	Proportion of the wingspan and the width of the wing (cord)
Back loop	Backwards rotation
Bindings	Wakeboard boots that attach the feet to the board
Blind	Riding backwards
Body drag	Being pulled by the kite in the water
Bottom turn	Changing direction at the bottom of the wave
Bridals	Lines that maintain the profile of the kite
Broad-reach	Riding between 110 and 140° from the wind direction
Close-hauled	Sailing direction to the wind (generally 70° to 45° to the wind)
Cord	Imaginary line connecting the front part of the kite's profile to the back (from one tip of a bladder to the next)
Course	A direction
Cross wind or reaching	Riding at an angle of 90° to the wind
Dead man	Aerial trick, head upside down, feet in the air, hands free
Deck	The top of the board
Delta kite	Kite in the shape of a triangle
Directional	Asymmetric shaped board with 2 or 3 footstraps and fins at the back
Downwind	What you see when the wind is to your back
Drag	Force created by the friction of the wind on the skin of the kite
Ebb	When the tide declines
Edging	Edge on the board with the toes or the heels, to change direction or manage the power
Flapping	When the kite waves like a flag
Flood	When the tide ascends
Footstrap	Strap that allows the kiteboarder's feet to stay on the board
Goofy	Person who uses his right foot as front foot (right foot forward)
Grab	When the rider catches the board during a jump
Handle pass	Passing the bar from one hand to the next behind the back and during a jump
Harness	Gear that you wear as a short or around the waist (seat or waist harness), with a hook connecting the rider to the harness line
Harness line	Rope covered with plastic, fixed to the bar, to attach oneself to the harness
Heart attack	Trick where the rider holds his board in one hand, has his feet in the air and the bar in the other hand
Heel stance	Position where the rider edges on his heels
Hull	Part of the board that is in the water

Practical tools

INTL. KITEBOARDING SIGNS

All riders should learn and use these signs in order to have a common language on the spot and avoid misinterpretations.

Place the kite at the top

Go this way

Go this way

I need help (with the bar, equipment problem)

Make a u-turn

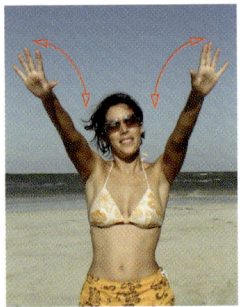
Let go of the bar

One hand patting head: I want to land (when the sign is done by a kiteboarder arriving to the shore)

One hand still: are you ok? Answer: yes, when used between two riders in the water or by a person on land

THE KNOTS

Below are the knots used for kiteboarding. They can also be used for many other purposes.

The figure 8 knot
The figure 8 knot (also called stopper or stop knot) is used to make connection points on the lines or the kite.

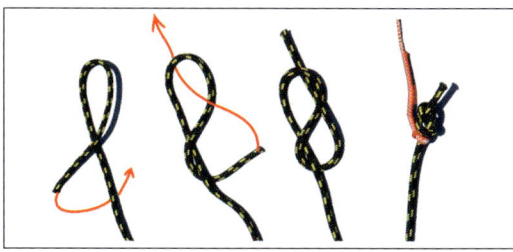

Double figure 8 knot
It is used to make loops that counteract traction, or to double the end of the lines to make another knot used to connect the lines to the kite.

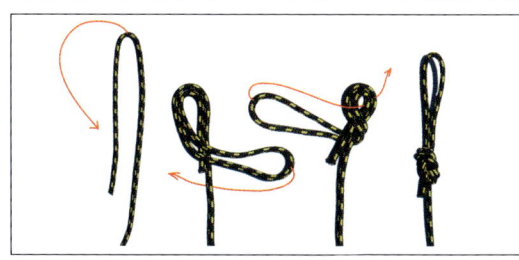

Larkshead knot
It is the knot that connects to the figure 8 knot. Always create a loop thanks to a double 8 knot.

Half hitch and stop knot
This knot is used to tie a rope on a loop or a part that has a small diameter, as for instance the power loop of the bar or the power strap.

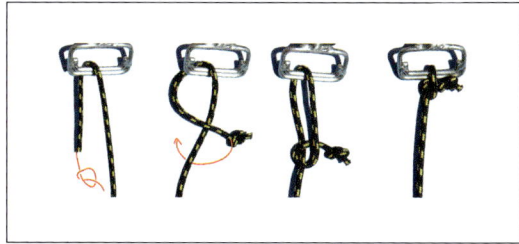

Bowline
Just as the half hitch knot, this knot is used to tie a rope on a loop. The advantage of this knot is that it is easily undone.

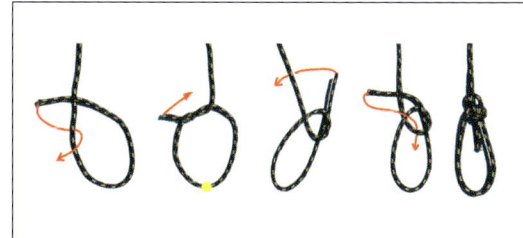

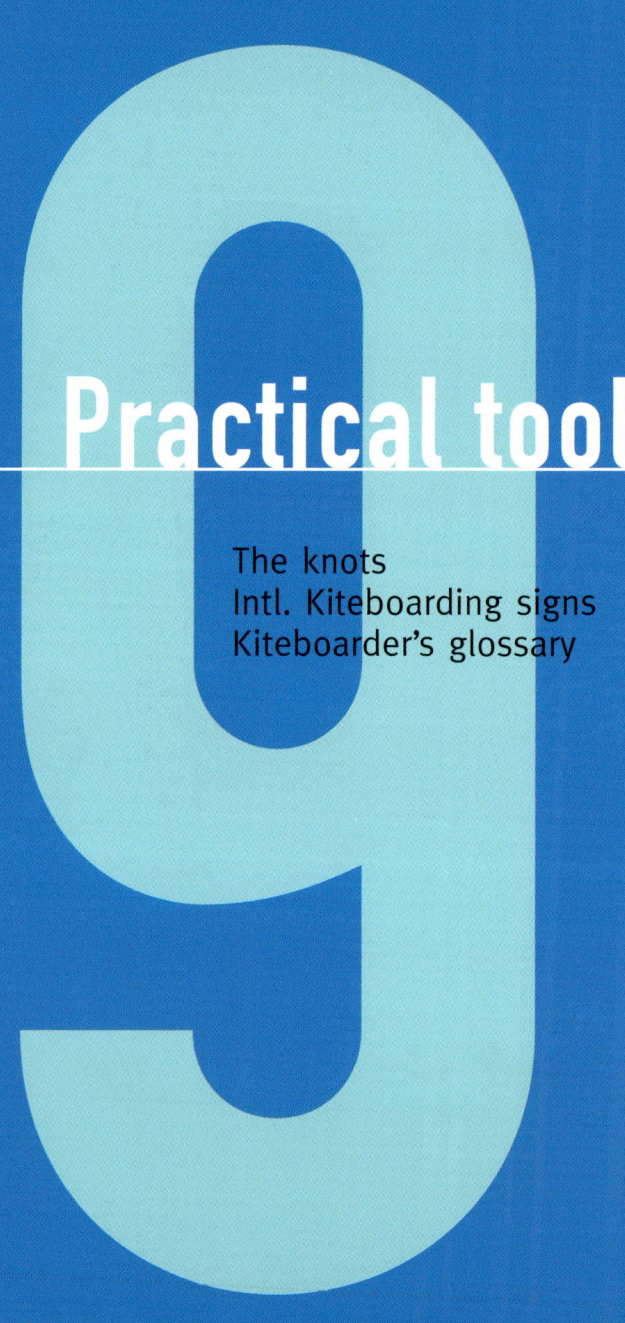

Practical tools

The knots
Intl. Kiteboarding signs
Kiteboarder's glossary

BUGGY

The buggy is steered with the feet. Seated close to the ground, it can go as fast as 60 to 80 km/h.
Buggy is usually practiced with foil kites on beaches where there is a low tide or on wide spaces, such as deserted airports of fields.

Whether you are on the water, on snow or on land, traction and piloting a kite is quite the same thing. Yet, the safety and practice rules specific to each of these sports must be understood by all riders. Ask for advice from qualified specialists and use the proper safety equipment.

The common point to all these sports is the kite. And even though some are more easy to use and better adapted, any type of kite can be used for these sports.

MOUNTAIN BOARD

Mountain board can be described as a skate board for all grounds. Mountain board can be practiced on a beach or in fields. The diameter of the wheels is about 15 cm and the board can be mounted with footstraps for jumps. It can be learnt and practiced with light wind. Yet the entire body must be protected (not like on this picture!).

SNOW KITE

Even though easy to set up and quite easy to pick up, you can quickly gain a lot of speed when snow kiting, which is why it is important to learn a few safety and wind rules that are specific to the practice on snow. For instance, you should never remove your surf board or ski before having landed your kite, otherwise you could get pulled without being able to exert any kind of resistance. You must also know what kite size to choose, which is not the same than for kiteboarding on water with the same wind.

Snow kite is practiced with a helmet to protect the chin, protections for the back, and elbows and knees pads.

Talk to specialists, never go out alone and give your itinerary to one of your friends. The distances you can travel can easily reach many kilometers.

Other Action Sports

8

The mountain board
Snow kite
Buggy

Meteorology

Beaufort scale

This scale is international. It gives visual references that make it possible to estimate the force of the wind and to have an international language.

The speed of the water is expressed in knots.
- 1 knot = 1 nautical mile covered in 1 hour
- 1 nautical mile = 1.852 km

For your information, it is advised to kiteboard in winds up to 25 knots with the proper equipment and skill level. Above that wind force, it is dangerous to kiteboard.

SEA DESCRIPTION	Scale in Beaufort	Wind speed in knots	Kiteboarder criterion
Sea like a mirror	0	0 to 1	Read a magazine
Few ripples	1	1 to 3	
Small wavelets	2	4 to 6	Try a 20m^2
Large wavelets, with few white caps	3	7 to 10	Prepare a 16m^2
Small waves, fairly frequent white caps	4	11 to 16	Perfect to kiteboard
Moderate waves, many white caps	5	17 to 21	Get ready for high jumps!
Large waves begin to form; white crests, probably spray	6	22 to 27	It's time to rig a smaller kite!
Sea heaps up and white foam blows in streaks along the direction of the wind	7	28 to 33	Time for the pros...
Medium waves, crests begin to break into spindrift	8	34 to 40	Forget kiteboarding!
High waves, dense foam along the direction of the wind. Crests of waves begin to roll over. Spray may affect visibility	9	41 to 47	
Very high waves with long overhanging crests. The surface of the sea takes a white appearance. Visibility affected	10	48 to 55	
Exceptionally high waves. The sea is completely covered with long white patches of foam lying in the direction of the wind. Visibility affected	11	56 to 63	
The air is filled with foam and spray. Sea completely white with driving spray. Poor visibility	12	+ 63	

Speed unit converter

1 knot	equals	0,514 m/s
1 knot		1,852 Km/h
1 m/s		1,95 knot
1 m/s		3,611 Km/h

Cumulonimbus

Not so rare and very powerful...

The cumulus, a little low white cloud, is not dangerous and remains calm until it turns into a cumulus congestius. When it turns into a cumulonimbus, it is really important to keep an eye on it and stay clear from it. Usually, it is best to stop kiteboarding.

The cumulonimbus can go upwind. It is therefore wrong to think that there is no risk because it is downwind. Take time to observe in which direction it is moving.

If it is upwind and/or moving towards you, land your kite. The wind can suddenly change direction and become very strong. If it starts to rain, a strong wind is generated (gust front). If you see rain upwind to you under a black cloud, go quickly to the shore because it can also create unpredictable lightening.

The cumulonimbus is characterized by its vertically developed shape and glaciated top that can extend to great heights. Usually, once it has passed, the wind drops or even stops completely and the cloud disappears.

Black sky

If the sky is black, chances are that the weather is going to change and there is going to be a storm. If the sky looks like the picture below, land your kite and wait until the cloud

has gone. You will usually see this kind of sky when there is a low pressure. Check out the weather forecast and local forecasts and wait until the cold front has passed to kiteboard with stable wind.

Using the barometer

Hurry! The wind is picking up! Look, the barometer is dropping quickly, let's go to the spot!

Whether it is a trade wind or a sea breeze, the wind picking up can be determined by the sudden drop of the barometer...

If the pressure drops	The wind
3 millibars in 3h	will be inferior or equal to 6 Beaufort
3 to 4 millibars in 3h	will strengthen up to 7 Beaufort
up to 7 millibars in 3h	will strengthen up to 8-9 Beaufort
more than 7 millibars in 3h	will strengthen up to 10 Beaufort

To your barometers!

Meteorology

What is the wind?

The wind can simply be defined as air in motion. This motion can come from any direction, but in most cases, the horizontal flow greatly exceeds the vertical wind flow. The wind speed can vary from absolute calm to speeds as high as 380 kilometers per hour (Mt. Washington, New Hampshire, 12th of April

1934). In 1894, strong winds in Nebraska pushed 6 cars, fully loaded with coal, on a distance of 160 kilometers in less than 3 hours. Wind is generated when there are spatial discrepancies in the atmospheric pressure.
Usually, these discrepancies are caused because of an uneven absorption of the solar radiations at the earth's surface. The wind speed seems to be at its greatest during daytime, when peaks in atmospheric temperature and pressure exist. The wind speed is measured in kilometers per hour (Km/h), miles per hour (M/h), knots or meters per second (M/s) and in Beaufort scale.

The sea breeze

Don't loose hope when there is no wind...
The high pressure is present, the sky is blue, but there is no wind. Yet, towards 11 o'clock, you see little clouds shaping above the sea and humid areas on the ground. They are cumulus of good weather. When the land is warm enough, the air on its surface is going to be lifted and replaced by the air of the sea that is cooler. During the day, this wind shift is called the see breeze (left hand drawing). The wind blows from the sea and is directed towards the land. This exchange occurs on the coast line. There is no wind in the open sea. The wind usually gets stronger late in the afternoon, then decreases until it drops

completely before night fall. The wind can then come back thanks to the opposite effect, because the air above the sea level is now warmer than on land (drawing above). During the day, the sea breeze blows onshore. During the night, it blows offshore.

The altitude effect

Altitude doesn't only affect our body. As the pressure goes down and we go higher, the air becomes less dense than the air at sea level. To be able to fly a kite with the same wind force, a kiteboarder will need a bigger kite size when in altitude.

Example: a rider weighs 75kg and rides with an $11m^2$ with 15 knots at sea level. With the same wind on the Titicaca Lake at an altitude of 3 810m, he needs a $15m^2$ kite to have the same power.
The difference in air density can also be felt at sea level because of the humidity.

You can determine how many meters the level of the water changes according to the ordinal of twelve rule:

For a 4m tide, divide 4 by 12=0.33 which results in 1/12=0.33m. Therefore 12/12=4 meters.

1st hour	1/12	0.33 x 1=0.33 m
2nd hour	2/12	0.33 x 2=0.66 m
3rd hour	3/12	0.33 x 3=0.99 m
4th hour	3/12	0.33 x 3=0.99 m
5th hour	2/12	0.33 x 2=0.66 m
6th hour	1/12	0.33 x 1=0.33 m

Using your knowledge on tides for kiteboarding

Check if the tide is flooding or ebbing and its coefficient. Determine if the current created by the tide is going against or in the same direction as the wind. If the current in against the wind, it will not be necessary to have a lot of power in the kite. When the current goes against the wind, there are wavelets on the water. On one hand, it will be very difficult to relaunch the kite from the water because the current might bring the kite towards you, consequently releasing the tension in the lines. On the other hand, if the current is moving in the same direction as the wind, you will need more power or stop kiteboarding and wait for the next tide. The water becomes glassy when the current goes in the same direction as the wind.

In some spots, you can kiteboard with a low tide; in others you can kiteboard with high tides. Ask the local riders for more information. If you start kiteboarding with a flood tide, make sure to stop riding before there is no more space left for you to land your kite. Check out the bottom of the sea for rocks or oyster beds at sea level or when the tide is low.
As for the tidal force, use the ordinal rule of twelve. There is less current during the first and last hour of the tide. If you choose to kiteboard at the beginning of the last hour of the flood or ebb tide, it will be followed by half an hour without current and then one hour with a slight current in the opposite direction. This will make it possible for you to kiteboard for about 2h30.

DISCOVER THE WEATHER

We usually watch the weather forecast on television. If that is where your knowledge rests, then this chapter has a few surprises in store for you.
Where does the wind come from, how can we determine if the wind will drop or get stronger, should the same kite size be used at sea level or on a lake in the mountains?
The answers follow, read them all, take your time and observe the clouds, the sea and the land each time you get ready to go kiteboarding. This valuable information that you are recording will help you assess if the conditions are favorable to go riding or not.

Meteorology

The spring tide is amplified by the gravitational attraction of the sun and the moon. Spring tides occur when the moon is at full phase or new phase. These two configurations correspond to the sun-earth-moon and sun-moon-earth alignments. In both cases, the gravitational forces of the sun and the moon act to reinforce each other, accounting for the amplified phenomenon.

With neap tides, the difference between the HW and the LW is small and similar to an average level called tide of diminished range (opposite drawing). The gravitation forces of the moon and of the sun are not at the same level.

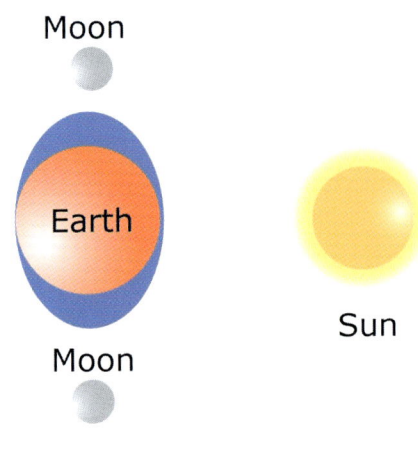

When the tide moves towards the shore, it is called flood. When the tide moves away from the shore, it is called ebb.

Realizing the distribution of tidal phases
The tide cycle is of 28 days during which the tides shift from spring to neap tides and then come back to spring tides.

Nevertheless, the tide cycle is affected by the local effects created by the coast and the underwater outline that influence the tidal wave. You need to check a tide directory (available on the internet or in most nautical sport shops) for more information. Each directory provides the time table for precise locations. The schedule also provides the tide's maximum and minimum height according to a specific coefficient. The bigger the coefficient, the bigger the difference in tidal height and the current movement.

An example of directory tide:

Coefficient	Time	Tide length	Height	Tide range	1/12	1/4	1/2
60	04h21 10h58	06h37	5,65m 2,09m	3,56m	0,3m	0,89m	1,78m

The ordinal rule of twelve
A tide lasts for 6 hours but its speed is influenced by the tide range. The level of the water changes faster at certain periods creating a stronger current during the 3rd and 4th hour of the tide.

Slower change		Faster change of the water level		Slower change	
1/12	2/12	3/12	3/12	2/12	1/12
1st hour	2nd hour	3rd hour	4th hour	5th hour	6th hour

113

THE TIDES

You have been kiteboarding for two hours and it is now time to come back to the shore. At that moment, you realize that the beach has disappeared! Usually, you can ride upwind, but today, you can't or on the contrary, without making any efforts, you can! A rock that you had never seen before suddenly appears in between waves. Your kite falls and regardless of the wind, the lines are slack because the tide is pushing the kite towards you...
All these cases are examples of situations that are due to the tide effects.

Principle

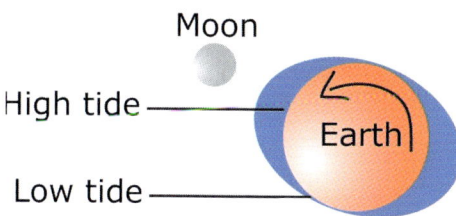

Tides are generated by the gravitational pull of the moon and the sun. Because the moon revolves around the earth, and the couple earth-moon revolve around the sun, external forces are exerted which draw the ocean's water masses on the earth's surface. A high or low tide lasts 6 hours with an interval of about 25 minutes during which the sea level does not change. The time schedule of tides is delayed by approximately 50 minutes per day. For example, if on Monday, the tide is low at 20:00 p.m., on the following Sunday, it will be low at 02:00 am. On the Atlantic coast, there are 2 high and 2 low tides per day.

Different locations, different tides

Tides can be diurnal or semidiurnal. A diurnal tide counts 2 low tides and 2 high tides per day, in other words a change every 6 hours. A semidiurnal tide counts 1 high and 1 low tide per day, in other words a change every 12 hours.

For example, in the Northern Pacific Ocean (America to Asia), the tides are diurnal. In the Indian Ocean, a semidiurnal system is confined in the south by a strip joining Australia to Somalia.
The range (difference in height between a low and high tide) of the diurnal tide is almost always small and never above 1 meter. The semidiurnal tide varies more and can reach 12 meters.

The smallest range can be observed in nearly closed seas. In the Black Sea, the range is almost inexistent. On the French Mediterranean coast, it ranges from 10 to 20 cm. In Haiti, the range reaches 0,4 meter and 1 meter in the Reunion Island.

There are two types of tides: neap and spring tides.

There are 2 neap tides and 2 spring tides in a month.

With the spring tide, the high waters (HW) are very high and the low waters (LW) very low (opposite drawing).
Two configurations of moon, earth and sun are responsible.

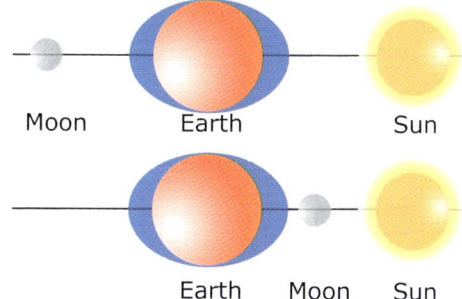

112

Meteorology

The tides
Discover the weather

From wind to traction

shorter. Therefore, the fact that there is less friction reduces the turbulence, allowing the air to flow on a larger surface. A low aspect ratio kite of the same surface generates less power because the airflow does not exert power, having covered only part of the profile, and creates turbulences and parasite forces.

- **The position of the connecting knots on the kite:** what it does mostly is influence the power management possibilities.
  Connection points that are closer together generally require more efforts in the arms to increase the power by pulling on the bar. A greater distance between the connection knots makes it easier to manage the power, but it also means that the arms are going to make bigger movements.
- **The weight:** a light kite can fly with less wind. The weight also influences the balance of the kite when it is positioned at the top of the wind window.

Changing parameters:
Changing parameters are the speed of the wind and the density of the air.

Changeable parameters:
The changeable parameters are the angle of attack of the kite with the power strap, the positioning of the bar on the leading line, the length of the lines, the speed of the kite in the wind window and the stances used on the board.

WHY CAN WE JUMP?

We jump thanks to the same principle used for the water start. When we fly the kite from one side of the wind window to the other, the power of the kite is added to the power in which we are going, because the power of the kite is directed towards the opposite direction. The addition of these forces is passed on in the kite that pulls upwards with a force superior to the weight of our body and that is why we take off.

Timing in regards to flying the kite and edging will make us go higher. Edging (in the water) at the moment we jump is important because the power of the kite also depends on the weight that is put on the lines thanks to the resistance created by the board in the water.
Every kite is different, so try training with the same kite in order to make progress and avoid using boards that skid a lot.

From wind to traction

Let's take an example with a downwind scenario: you are riding downwind, in other words in the same direction as the wind. The wind is blowing at 10 knots. You are moving at a speed of 5 knots.
10 − 5 = 5, so you feel a wind force of 5 knots. In this case scenario, it is the apparent wind.

The apparent wind can also be stronger than the true wind.
Let's take another example: the wind is still blowing at 10 knots and you are moving at a speed of 5 knots against the wind. 10 + 5 = 15. You feel a wind force of 15 knots.

Observing the apparent wind

You can observe the effect of the apparent wind when you kiteboard by checking out if your kite is moving forward or backward at the wind window's edge.

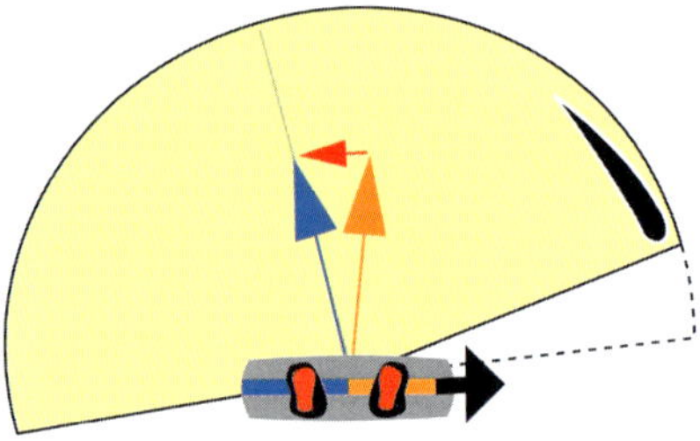

The faster you go, the more your kite will move backwards. Most kiteboarders say that the kite goes in the wind window. In fact, it remains at the edge of the wind window but the wind window turns to remain in the line of the apparent wind (opposite drawing, blue arrow).

The effects of the apparent wind are the following:
- When you go fast, keep your board flat on the water and move the kite up and down, the kite moves backwards and the angle between the board and the lines is bigger (opposite drawing). It becomes harder to take an edge and go upwind. You must anticipate and edge on your heels sooner before you have too much speed.

On the other hand, with little speed, meaning little apparent wind, it's not possible to stand on the board.

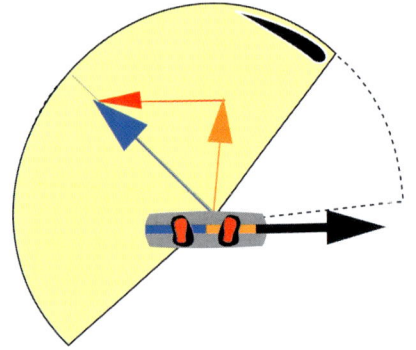

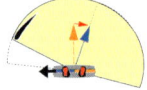  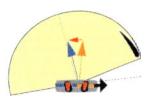

The effects of the apparent wind when we move to the right or to the left

Parameters that influence the power of the kite

Fixed parameters:
- **The design of the kite**: the round profile gives the kite stability and provides easy power management. The flat profile is more performant but also more sensitive to the change of angle according to the force of the wind. In turn, this requires more precision while flying the kite to manage the power.
- **The aspect ratio**: it influences the circulation of the airflow. A high aspect ratio creates less turbulence because the distance between the leading and trailing edge is

Power of the kite

These notions must be remembered: the power of the kite is relative to the speed of the wind that is exerted on its surface. Yet double the speed does not result in double the power but 4 times more.

This is what causes traction, either when the kite passes in the middle of the wind window, when we fly the kite to make a jump, or simply when we have a little speed once on the board. The power is therefore proportional to the speed multiplied by itself.

A kite does not pull much when it flies at the edge of the wind window (above your head or on the sides). But as soon as it gains speed, either by passing through the power window, either because the pilot is in motion, its power greatly increases.

If this is all Chinese to you, then here's an example.

In the power zone, a 5m² kite produces a power of 50kg with wind blowing at 10 knots. The same kite produces a power of 200kg with wind blowing at 20 knots.
2 times more wind = 4 times more power.

Note: The vectors on the following drawing illustrate the power that is exerted on the kite and not the power developed by the kite.

The power of the kite is strongest when the kite passes in the middle of the power window because the apparent wind (blue arrow) is the most powerful at that moment, and it has an angle that allows optimum air flow on the profile of the kite. You feel this power when you are on land or when you do a water start.

Example: the kite passes from the right to

the left, the kite pilot does not move. The power (in blue) is the apparent wind. Notice that the apparent wind is proportional to the velocity wind (red arrow).

The power in movement

Apparent wind
The apparent wind is the wind that we feel when we are in motion.
It is made out of the true wind (the one that we feel when we are not in motion, orange arrow) and of the velocity wind. The velocity wind is created by the motion. It is proportionate to the speed but in the opposite direction (red on the drawing).

The apparent wind plays an important part in the upwind performance and power management. To go upwind, the rider must go slower than the true wind, otherwise the apparent wind will not be oriented correctly. The following drawing will help you understand.

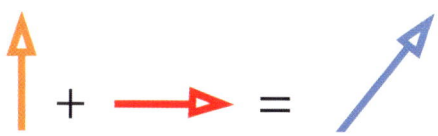

Apparent wind (blue) = true wind (orange) + velocity wind (red).

From wind to traction

The intrados
It is the interior of the kite's profile.

The extrados
It is the exterior of the kite's profile.

The shapes of a kite

A Delta
B Rectangular
C Semi elliptic
D Elliptic
E Semi elliptic with a negative trailing edge

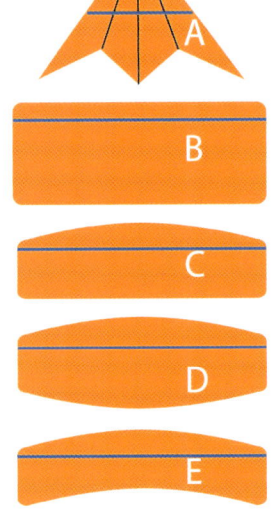

The elliptic shape is the most commonly used because it allows, among other things, to put the pig tail knots opposite the forces exerted by the kite, giving more adjustment possibilities and better feelings when piloting the kite.

The canopy shape

It is the curve of a kite seen face on. This curve gives stability to the kite when it is moving because the canopy shape channels the air. The canopy shape can be either central as on inflatable kites or spread on the entire length as on arched kites. This is the reason why inflatable kites are so stable.

The profile

The profile affects the performance of the kite.

A very flat profile is very fast, but very sensitive to wind changes or to the action of the pilot on the angle of attack.

A very curved profile makes the kite stable and easy to sheet in and out.
Yet this type of profile is very slow because it generates extra drag.

The pitch
It is the ratio between the position of the front line connection knots and the points where the power of the kite is exerted (green arrow). The pitch influences the balance between the kite and its abilities to sheet in or out by changing the angle of attack.

According to the profile and the type of kite, the center of pressure is more or less positioned at the front, which influences the position of the front line connection knots.

Traction terminology

The cord
It is the line that passes from the center of the kite's profile. This line defines the angle of attack and the width of the profile (white dots).

The drag
It is the force developed by the friction of the air on the kite and of the wake created as the wind passes on the profile. This force always moves in the same direction as the wind on the kite (black arrow).

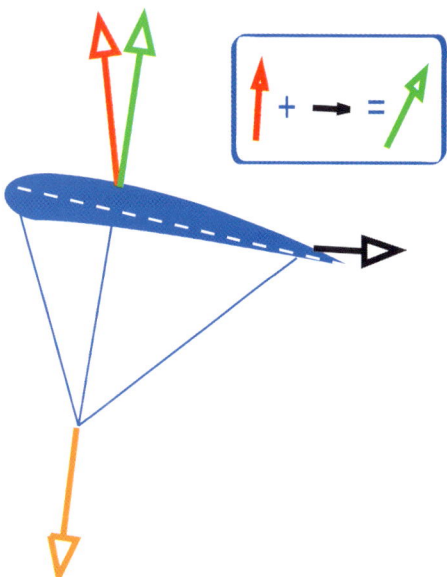

The lift
It is the force created by the passage of the air on the profile of the kite (red arrow).

The aerodynamic force
It is the total amount of force created on the kite, either by the lift or by the drag.
Designers are of course looking for ways to reduce the drag in favor of the aerodynamic force, which will consequently be better oriented for upwind performances (green arrow).

The weight
It is the force exerted by the weight of the pilot when he is on land. The resistance of the board when the kiteboarder is in the water can be added to this force (orange arrow).

The angle of attack
It is the angle between the cord of the kite and the wind. Changing angle of attack affects the power of the kite. You change this angle by using the bar or the power strap fixed on the leader line. With a small angle, the profile creates a sufficient force for the kite to stay in the air. With more angle, the kite powers up more. With too much angle, the drag becomes stronger and the kite is pulled backwards.

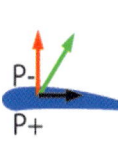 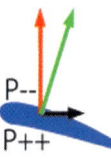 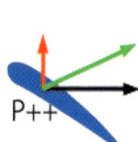

This drawing is only an example. The forces vary according to the profile of the kite, the type of kite (foil or inflatable) and the angle of attack.

The leading edge
It is the part of the kite that is in contact with the wind first, the thickest part of the kite.

The trailing edge
It is the end of the kite, the thinnest part.

From wind to traction

A plane profile (NACA) prevents the creation of wake and favors the creation of the lift.

The vortex is a whirlwind that is created on the tip of the kite as the wind that goes over the sail (extrados) and the wind that goes under it (intrados) meet.

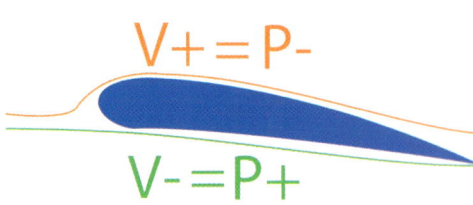

Why does a kite fly and pull?

The airflow is separated when it meets the kite, as air goes under and over it.
The airflow then covers two different distances, but arrives at the same time. The wind that is over (extrados) the kite (orange on the opposite drawing) has to go faster, which creates a power that pulls the kite upwards. The wind that is under (intrados) slows down slightly, and creates a power that pushes the kite (green on the opposite drawing). This only works if the kite has an adapted shape, like a plane wing, and if the wind blows into the kite at an average angle of 15 to 25°.

When the speed (S) of the wind over the kite increases, its pressure (P) decreases (S + = P -). A negative pressure is then exerted on the surface of the profile, which lifts it upwards (orange airflow).

When the speed of the wind decreases on a profile (S-) the pressure increases (P+), which pushes the profile. The forces exerted with pressure (green airflow) represent 25% of the total power exerted on the profile. The forces that actually draw in represent 75%. Just like an airplane wing, a kiteboarding wing flies thanks to the decrease of pressure on its extrados.

The forces that are produced vary according to the angle between the kite and the wind. The drawings show the passage of the air stripes according to the angle between the kite and the wind (angle of attack). The larger the angle of attack, the greater the turbulences.

Consequently, it is useless to pull too much on your bar to increase the power.

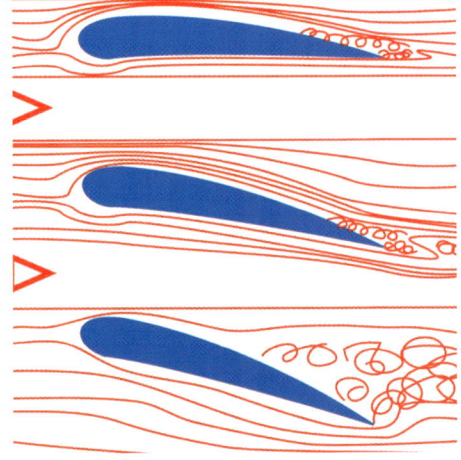

Traction is created by the speed of the wind on the kite. The power is therefore created by piloting the kite from one side of the wind window to the other when we are at a halt, and by the wind created by the acquired speed once we are standing on the board and kiteboarding. It is therefore important to manage the speed and especially not to slow down too much, unless you want to stop and do a water start.

THE LENGTH OF THE LINES

We usually use 25 to 30 meter lines, which gives the kite enough range in the wind window. It also gives the pilot enough time to anticipate his moves.
The advantage of using 15 to 20 meter lines is to be able to manage more power by exerting more pressure on the board. Piloting becomes more sensitive and taking off during jumps faster. Yet, with the first piloting mistake, the kite will make a loop in the power window and create a strong pull. This is a trick called the kite loop, but it is very dangerous if it is done involuntarily.

Why not with 70m lines?

The friction of the wind on 70m lines is so great that the lines act as shock absorbers and the bar has nearly no more control over the kite. Going upwind is very difficult since the power of the kite is not well oriented with the board.

AERODYNAMICS

This chapter will help you understand the basics of a kite's aerodynamics.

The air and the shapes

To have traction, there must be a shape and air in motion on this shape. This creates friction and pressure also called negative pres-

sure. The addition of all these forces exerted on the shape creates traction.
According to the profile of this shape and its angle according to the wind, the force created will be more or less important.

Opposite is a picture of the test of a kite in a blower. The green fabrics allow visualizing the passage of the air on the profile of the kite.

The square and the circle cause too much wake to create a usable force.

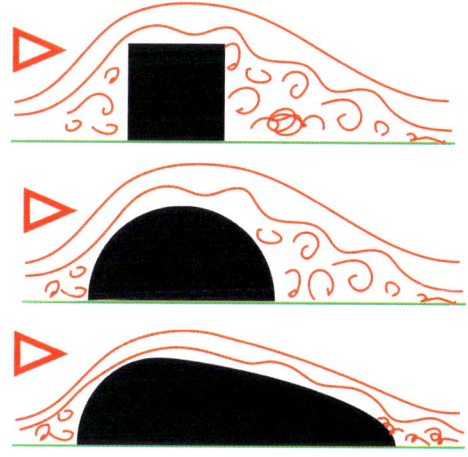

From wind to traction

The length of the lines
Aerodynamics
Why can we jump?

Improvement

EVOLUTION

It's up to you to observe and invent tricks by mixing the ones presented above. For instance, you can make a back loop and land it blind, ride blind and do a back loop or a tantrum, make a board off with an invert... Add a few grabs and you've got it!

A trampoline course, simulating in the water, or hanging from a bar on land and working on the positions and transitions will help you to improve.

Visualize the tricks before attempting them.

Opposite picture: handle pass with an invert (passing of the bar from one hand to the other behind the back, head upside down).

THE DEAD MAN

It is the same principle as the jump head upside down but before completing your ascent, let go of the bar and stretch your arms behind your head or put your hands on your neck. To avoid coming down too fast and miss your landing, you must either hook into the harness, or use the power trim to add power.

THE TANTRUM

The tantrum is a front rotation, just like the front loop, but the front hand is placed on the bar and the shoulders rotate at 90°.
Turn frontwards the moment you jump, and turn your back to the direction in which you are going.

NO FOOT OR BOARD OFF

Your board must have a handle placed at the center. Jump, bend your knees, grab the board, and take your feet out of the straps. At that moment you can stretch your legs for extra style. Then quickly bend and bring the board back to your knees, while keeping the kite at 12 o'clock.

You can also change your body position. This trick is called a heart attack (picture above).

Improvement

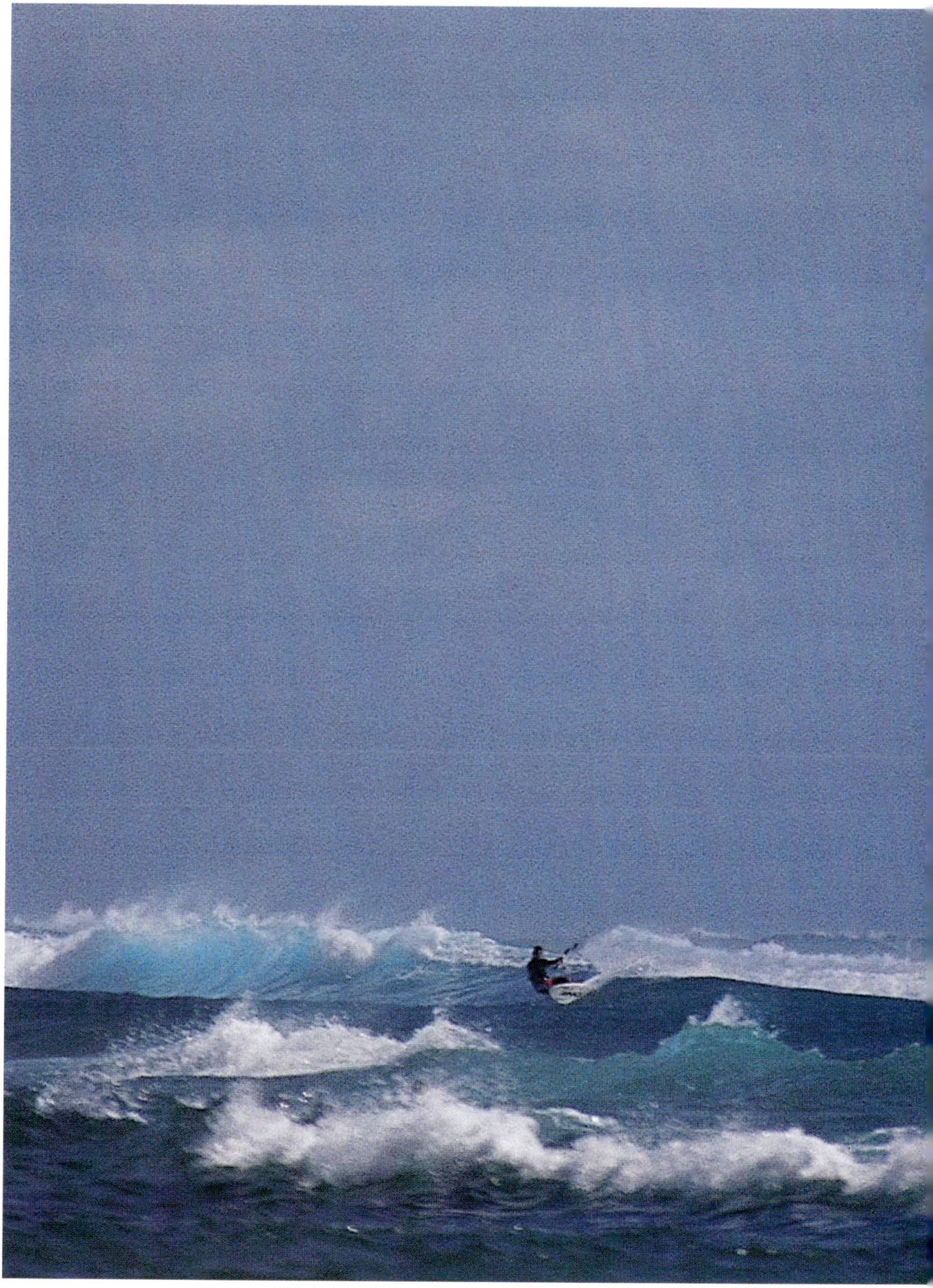

Improvement

BACKWARD 360° WITH A CHANGE OF DIRECTION

To try this trick, you must be able to do a simple back loop.

It's the same principle as for a back loop. The difference is that you are going to edge and slow down before jumping, which will also help the rotation.

- Instead of piloting the kite to bring it back to its initial position in the middle of the rotation, continue to fly the kite without changing its course in order to keep the kite at the other side of the wind window.

- Then put the board downwind in the new direction, opposite the one that you had at the moment of the jump.

360° FRONT ROTATION

On land, practice twirling. The moment you have to jump, swing your arms on the side you are going to turn.

On the water, the moment you take off, throw your front shoulder frontwards. Half way through the rotation, turn your head over your back shoulder to the original direction to spot your landing and let your body follow your head.

Don't forget to fly your kite forward as you come around for the landing.

FRONT LOOP

Use the same method as for the 360° front rotation. The difference is that once in the air, move your chest up and your legs down.

Put your back hand at the center of the bar to help the rotation and the piloting.

JUMPING HEAD UPSIDE DOWN (INVERTED)

Make a normal jump, but the moment you take off, swing your head and chest backwards.
To help your body move into an inverted position quickly and effortlessly, bend your legs (bring the board closer to your bottom). Once upside down, all you need to do is stretch your legs. To come back right side out, bend your chest and keep your legs stretched. The impulse of the chest is enough to bring you back right side out.

With practice, you will improve this jump by totally stretching your body and your arms.
You can also elaborate this jump with a back hand grab or landing in the opposite direction.

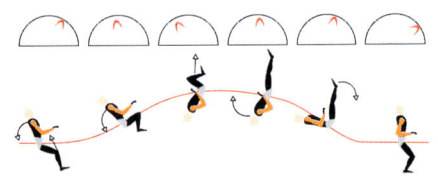

THE GRABS

The simple grab

It's about grabbing the back, front or middle of the board.
Bend your legs to make it easier to grab the board. You can then stretch a leg or make the board swing with one hand. Using the harness line helps staying in the air, but you can also increase the power of the kite by adjusting the power trim.

One foot jumps

You have to be able to jump, fly the kite with one hand, and grab the board. Once in the air, grab the board either at the edge or the rail, depending on your style and flexibility.
Remove one foot from the strap and stretch your leg either over or behind the board. As soon as you start piloting your kite to land, put your foot back into the strap. You must be able to fly the kite without looking at it because you will be concentrating on your foot until you have mastered the movement.
Large footstraps make this maneuver easier.

Improvement

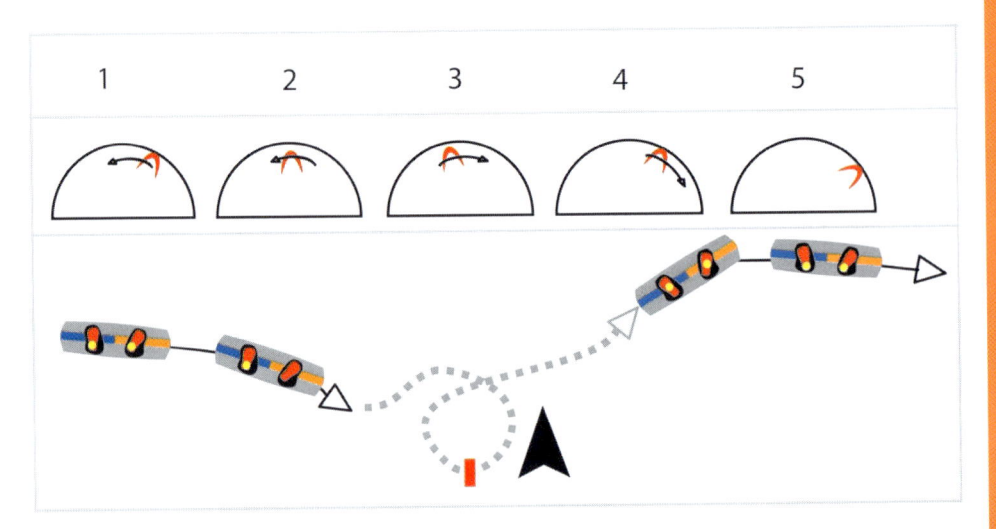

Improving the back loop (360°)

To improve the rotation, it is important to use your shoulders, head, and hips.
Once you have completed half a turn, try to look into the direction you must go after the landing.
Shoulders and elbows can also help regain balance after a jump.

What is more impressive and artistic is a back loop with your head upside down and your legs stretched towards the kite. To do that, you must be able to jump high and for a long time.

To put your body upside down, bend your knees once you have started turning, and throw your chest backwards. The heaviest part of your body becomes your chest. Once upside down, stretch your legs (you must be at half a turn). At that moment, pull on the opposite hand than the one used to take off, turn your head and bend your chest to complete the turn. The legs become the heaviest part of the body and you come back right side up.

You can simulate the move by hanging from a tree before trying it on the water.

Remember! You must be able to manage simple jumps before reaching this point if you don't want to suffer from rough landings!
For safety reasons, use a flotation or impact vest and a helmet.

Make many turns during the back loop

Increase the speed of the edging. The height of the jump and keeping your body together will make you turn more.

To make two turns (720°), start piloting the kite back when you have done 1 turn.

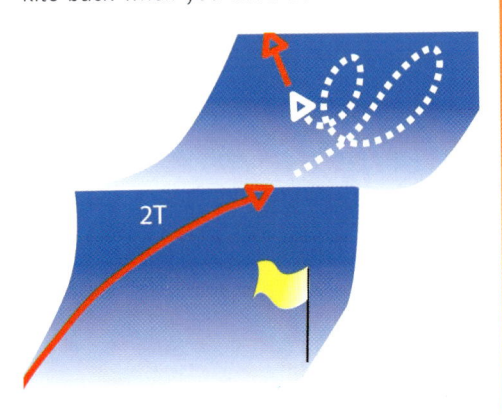

THE BACK LOOP

The first transitions are the ones that you do backwards. The back loop is the simplest transition and the basis to learn most of the other backward transitions.
Basic rotations that will help you learn more complex tricks are described later.
The blue drawing represents the path to follow on a wave to do a back loop.

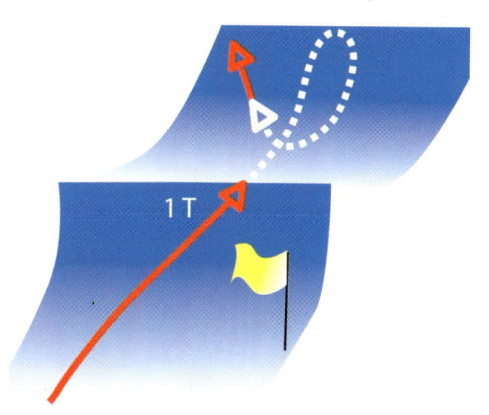

Steps 1 and 2
The bigger the wave, the less you need to edge heel side to complete only one turn. To turn two or three times, you need to edge more heel side and keep your body together.

- Fly the kite at 12 o'clock.
- The board: go upwind, edge and put weight at the back of the board to start the rotation.

Step 3
- As you are half-way through the rotation, fly the kite back to its starting position.

Step 4
- Direct the board downwind in order not to fall during the landing and continue piloting the kite towards the water.

Step 5
- Edge heel side to go upwind before gaining too much speed.

Improvement

4. Recover your sailing position by pushing on your front foot and slightly lifting your back foot.
5. Regain speed and the desired direction.

I fall backwards

You are edging too much heel side or you are looking into the direction in which you are going: look behind you and then adjust your body position.

I slow down and stop

You are putting too much pressure on your toes or on the foot that is at the back (according to the direction in which you are moving). Another reason could be that you don't have enough power.

THE JUMP WITH A TRANSITION

Landing a jump in the opposite direction is like changing direction on a twin tip or wakeboard. You need to simultaneously fly the kite faster and maintain speed in order to jump during the change of direction.
To land a high jump in the opposite direction, maintain the kite at around 12 o'clock and fly it quickly in the desired direction right before landing.

THE LONG JUMP

A lot of speed is needed for this jump. Edge less heel side and put the kite very high in the wind window. You must fly the kite quickly to 12 o'clock. This is not a hard jump but it requires good control of the board with speed. The kite must remain at 12 o'clock until the landing.

THE HIGH JUMP

Speed, good edging, and piloting the kite backwards as you are going towards the right are the prerequisites for this trick. Fly the kite from 2 to 10 o'clock with power and speed in order to bring the kite back to a sailing position at 1 o'clock. During this jump, the kite will slightly lift you a second time before landing. Keep your legs together and use your head and your shoulders to regain balance if necessary.

A wave will help you go higher if you jump the moment you meet the wave.

I slide and fall backwards when I land

That means you are landing with the board perpendicular to the wind or even upwind. You must direct the board downwind, position it flatter and edge as soon as you touch the water. Landing while directing the board downwind increases stability during landing but it also makes you loose speed. Once you are able to land your jumps, you will have to reposition the kite at the bottom of the wind window right after the landing to compensate for the loss of speed.

I go fast, but not high

You are probably going too much down wind. Exert heel side pressure, especially on your back foot, before starting your jumps.

THE TRICKS

Many sports, such as wakeboard, snow board and skate board, have influenced the practice of kiteboarding. Nevertheless, the sport is constantly evolving, and the professional riders often invent new tricks. Far from being complete, here is a list of possible tricks that can be considered as a base to make progress from.

BLIND OR BACKWARDS

Going blind is simply riding backwards toe side. Although this is an impressive trick, it is also an easy one to learn. What you need to do is first learn to ride toe side.

1. With speed, position the kite a little higher than at half of the wind window.

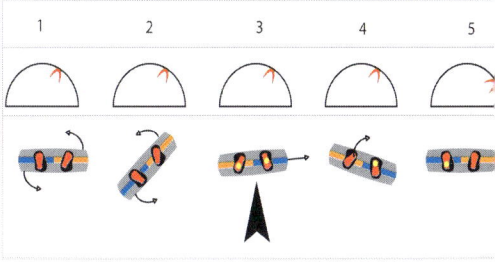

   Before doing that, let go of your back hand and put the other hand at the center of the bar.
2. Jump without using the kite and change the direction of your body and board.
3. Once you have passed this step, work on your stances. To progress, don't look into the direction you are going but rather into the opposite one, towards the horizon.

Improvement

IMPROVING YOUR JUMP

In a perfect world, everything works with the first go, but it's not the case in the real world. You are having problems completing your jump? Don't worry, it's normal.
The following cases describe the common difficulties most kiteboarders meet. They all have their solutions.
You will do better next time for sure.

I hardly take off

You are either underpowered or piloting the kite too slowly. Small jumps are also due to a lack of edging before taking off and to a bad coordination between the edging and piloting the kite backwards.
Make sure you have speed without going too fast and make sure to edge really hard right before being lifted by the kite. Work on the piloting and edging separately in order to be able to understand their effects. Don't hesitate to fly the kite quickly but be careful not to bring it completely on the other side of the wind window.

The kite falls when I land

Congratulations, you have passed the step of the first jumps. If your kite falls at the exact moment you touch the water, it is because the power is no longer exerted on your kite but on your descent. The apparent wind instantly changes direction, touches the exterior of the kite (extrados) and makes it stall and fall. This means that you are keeping the kite too long in a parachute position above your head. You must anticipate this and fly the kite more firmly forward to bring it back to a power position before landing.

I involuntarily start a turn while taking off

You are probably pushing too hard heel side when you take off. Lock your ankle position and your front and back stances right before the kite lifts you up.

Turning your head or moving a shoulder backwards and the other forwards can trigger a turn once you are in the air.

The principle of the jump

The principle of the jump is to use the power of the kite by piloting it towards the top and by adding the cruising speed to its force.
Think of these three steps to learn and look at your kite:

- (1,2) the take off
- (3)   the jump
- (4,5) the landing

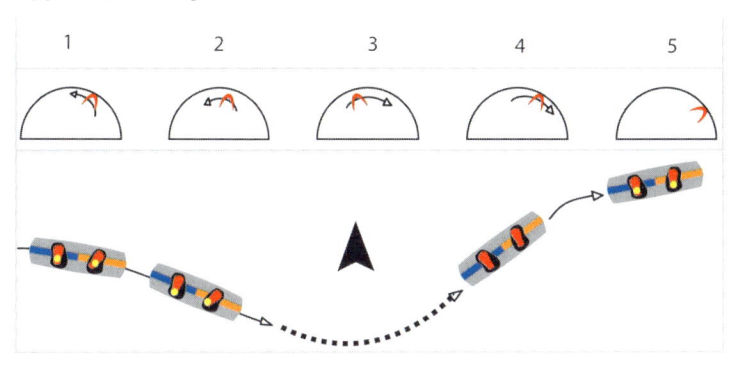

The take off
The easiest way is to go fairly fast at 90° according to the wind, the kite positioned at half the height of the wind window or a bit higher. Then take a good edge (heel side) while quickly piloting the kite towards the top as described in figures 1 and 2.
The trick is to coordinate the edging and the position of the kite to have the maximum traction towards the top.
Piloting the kite quickly depends on the size and type of the kite. Stop edging when you feel that the kite is pulling you upwards.
With experience, you will also be able to jump when riding broad-reach (board at approximately 45° to the wind).

The jump
Right after the jump, you must bare in mind that if you keep the kite in the same position, it will not be possible to land softly.

Therefore, after the take off, put your kite above your head by placing the bar parallel to the water. Use the kite like a parachute and bend your legs to balance yourself once in the air. This step can be disregarded if the jump is small. For your first jumps, think of bringing the kite back to a piloting position immediately after the take off (drawing 3).

The landing
It is harder to land than to jump but it is nicer. The final touch of a jump is a successful landing.
The higher you jump, the later you will pilot the kite back to its original position. This is done as you start coming back down. To make landing easier, place your board down wind (drawings 4 & 5).

You will achieve the proper rhythm with time and training. Don't hesitate to be quick in the piloting move that will make you take off.

Safety advice
- Never jump while using a board leash.
- Never let go of the bar when you are in the air.
- Try jumping on a wave, it is easier.
- Accelerate enough before jumping, but not too much.
- If you feel that the landing is going to be rough, kick the board away and place the kite above your head.
- Wear a helmet.
- Once in the air, bend your legs under your bar. This will help you position yourself for the landing, maintain balance while in the air, and avoid landing on your back.

Improvement

To surf a wave, you must be able to control your speed, meaning you must be able to slow down to stay on the wave and use its power rather than the power of the kite. Use a small size kite to avoid having too much power as you are using the wave as an additional power.

The point is to move up and down on the wave. A turn at the bottom of the wave is called a "bottom turn" and a turn on the lip is called an "off the lip".

Once more, the notion of stances mentioned previously is important. Push on the front to accelerate the moment you get on the wave, or else the wave will pass before you. Use the back stance to reduce the radius of your turns to stay on the wave or let it catch up with you to stop surfing.

If you fall, fly the kite in the opposite direction from the wave to prevent the kite from falling. If you keep the kite in the same direction, your body will continue to move with the wave and your lines will loose tension. Consequently, you will loose control of your kite and it will fall.

For the kite to relaunch on waves, it must be rigid, in other words well inflated.

THE FIRST JUMP

Being able to fly above the water is one of the great pleasures of kiteboarding.
But jumping is not the term that corresponds to the technical reality. It is more a matter of taking off thanks to the power of the kite. You can jump on flat water or with the help of waves. Everyone can do it! Fear put aside, the technical advice that follows is enough to guide you to your first take off!

A jump usually lasts 2 to 5 seconds, but the experienced competitors jump for around 10 seconds. The evolution in equipment will certainly make this air time increase even more.

Time for your first jump!
The first thing you must be able to do is ride with power and maintain an edge. Learn at your own rhythm, progressively pass the steps , and train only in the water, away from the shore.

Jibe by changing the feet before turning
1. Press on your toes to bring the board flatter on the water
2. Move the heel of the front foot towards the inside of the board to let the other foot reach the other footstrap
3. Remove the back foot, put it between the back footstrap and the other foot, then in the available front footstrap
4. After putting the back foot in the footstrap, put the foot that was at the front on the nonskid surface. At that precise moment, you are kiteboarding toe side
5. Fly the kite in the opposite direction and exert heel side pressure at the back of the board while making sure you don't fly the kite too fast in the other direction

Different scenarios

I fall downwind or I am lifted by the kite
You edge toe side too late, you must start turning by using your toes sooner.

I change direction and feet but I completely loose speed
You don't turn enough or turn too late. Keep your weight at the back of the board as soon as you have completed half the turn. To turn faster, edge more and complete your turn with the board before the kite is at the other side of the window.

RIDING TOE SIDE

It's one of the first tricks you can do and it is completely risk free. The purpose is to put the front of the board at the back and end up edging toe side instead of the heel side.
If you are right-handed, the easiest way is to go to the left while piloting the kite. All you'll have to do is to press on the front of the board and put your back foot at the front.

SURFING A WAVE

Surfing is a unique feeling. Imagine that you are kiteboarding, and behind you, a wave swells up. You edge slightly heel side to slow down, until you have coordinated your speed to the speed of the wave. Slow down a little more until you find yourself at half the height of the wave. Then press on the front of the board to go faster and there you are, surfing. The power of the wave almost replaces the kite's power. The feeling is great. You are playing with a wall of water in motion. It's possible, and you can do it!

To get a hang of the feeling, start with little waves or swells. Learn how to manage your stress. Keeping self control is important. If you are caught under a wave, it will help you to calmly wait and regain your breath once out of the water instead of swallowing a mouthful. Watch the waves and always make sure you can move away if necessary.

Improvement

because you won't be able to reach your board. Pull on the power trim to release power if necessary (if you are using a 4 line system).

THE JIBE

There are two types of jibes you can do on a directional or a mutant board.
The first one consists in changing the side of the feet before turning. The second one consists in changing the side of the feet during or after the turn. In both cases, the kite changes direction when the board starts to turn, but the turn of the board must be completed before the kite moves to the other side of the wind window.
Changing the feet position before turning gives the advantage of not loosing balance during the maneuver, but requires knowing how to ride toe side.

The two ways to jibe

Jibe by changing the feet during or after the turn
1. Remove the back foot from the footstrap, put it in front of the back footstrap, and flatten the board by pressing on your toes
2. Move the heel of the front foot towards the inside of the board so that the other foot can easily move to the other footstrap and exert toe side pressure with your back foot
3. Put your back foot in the available front foot strap and continue edging on it once in place
4. Right after placing the back foot in the front strap, remove your front foot from the strap and put it on the nonskid surface
5. Continue to push on the same side of the board using your heels and put your other foot in the back foot strap
6. Look in the direction you wish to go

The drawing describes the feet, the stances and the position of the kite according to the board.

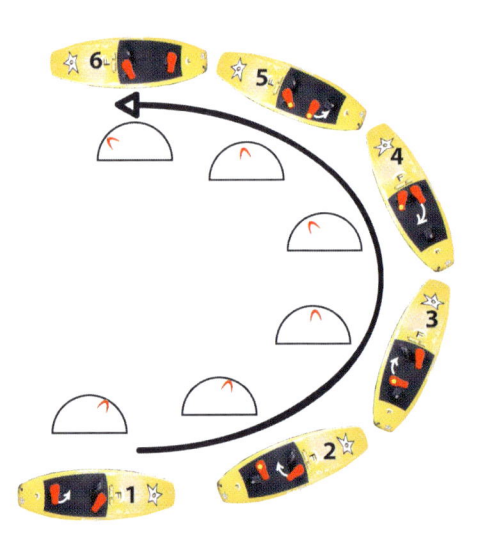

CHANGING DIRECTION WITH A TWIN TIP

To change direction, you must coordinate the movement of the board and the kite well. Changing direction can be split into 3 distinctive steps: slowing down with the help of the board, changing the direction of the kite and regaining speed.

First the board
1. Your back leg must be slightly bent
2. Stretch it by pushing heel side. The board must slide a little

Tip: train slidding the board by pushing backwards while continuing to go forwards.

Then the kite
3. Fly the kite in the opposite direction from the one you are headed in. Slightly bend your back leg (your right leg in the picture above)
4. Push on your back leg to loose speed and then fly the kite faster in the opposite direction
5. Press on your front leg to regain speed
6. Press on your back foot to control the speed as soon as you have regained it

Tip: follow the kite with your hips.

If you fall backwards, it is because you are piloting the kite too slowly or you lean too much backwards. If you are lifted above the water, you are piloting the kite too quickly from one side to the other.

If the kite changes direction but you don't, it's because you forgot to edge heel side.

BODY DRAGGING UPWIND

When you kiteboard without a board leash or if it is broken, you have to recover your board. Lay your body on the side, put the kite at half the height on the side of the wind window. Swim to the wind with your legs and one arm stretched in the water. Move at least 10 meters away from your board then slowly change direction. Remain in the lying position and repeat the same thing in that direction.

Be careful not to have too much power

Improvement

Change of direction with a twin tip
Body dragging upwind
The jibe
Riding toe side
Surfing a wave
The first jump
Improving your jump
The tricks
Blind or backwards
The jump with a transition
The long jump
The high jump
The back loop
The grabs
Backwards 360° with change of direction
360° front rotation
Front loop
Jumping head upside down (inverted)
The dead man
The tantrum
No foot or board off
Evolution

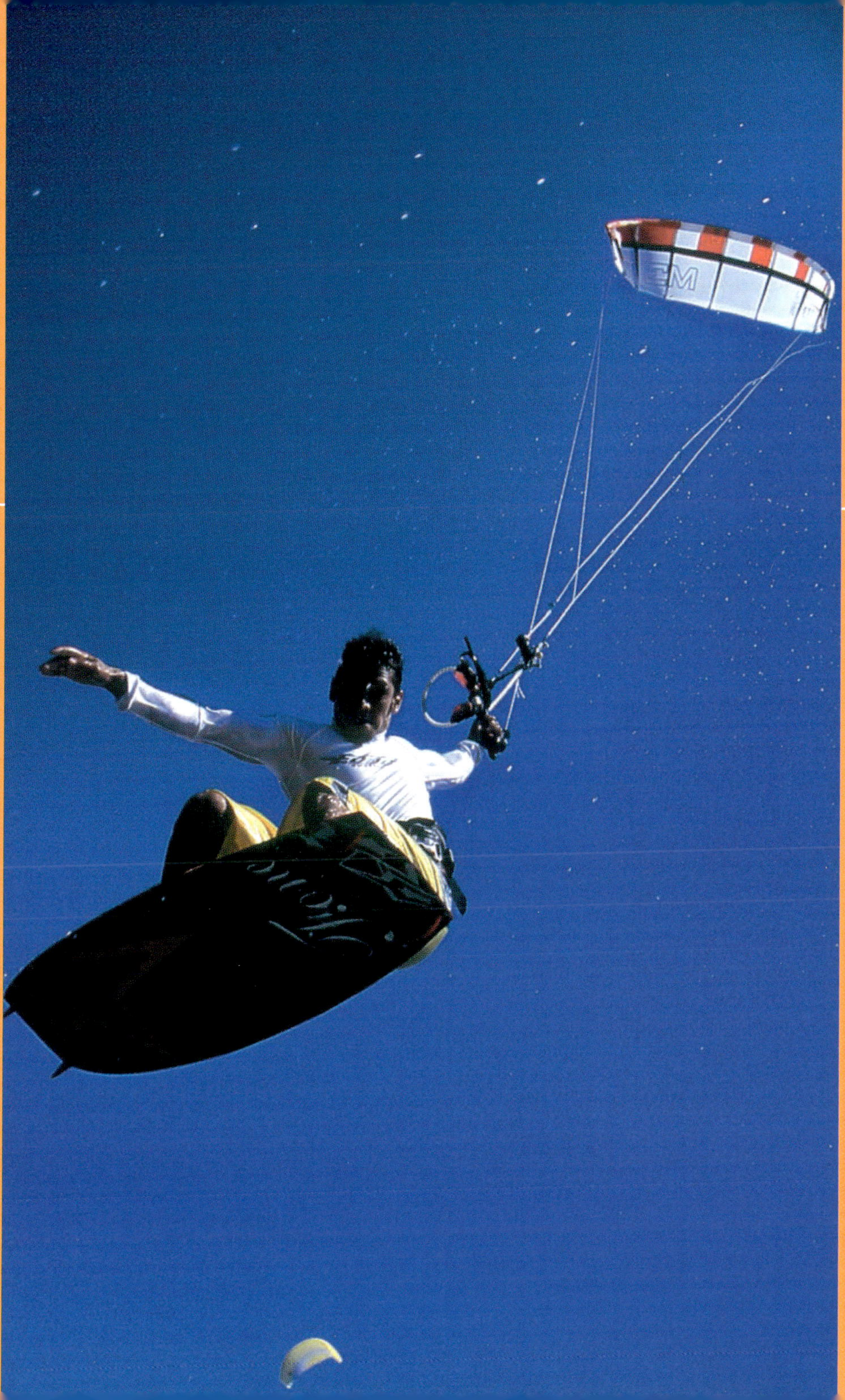

Practice

EQUIPMENT TIPS

The lines are tangled

If the bar has not made a turn in the lines, don't disconnect them from the kite. The entanglement is due to numerous loops that you need to undo.

A knot in the lines

Pull on the fiber one by one with a needle or use tweezers to undo the knot. Verify the line is in a good condition before using it.

Tip not to damage the kite

Put sand on the trailing edge when you leave your kite on the beach and don't let it in the sun more than 5 minutes. Rinse it and store it in its bag. Don't drag it on the ground, carry it. Don't let it fall heavily in the water or on the ground.

A little hole of maximum 2 cm in the board

Use an epoxy sealer, usually a 2 stick component that you will find in most shops. Remove the paint with a knife around the damaged area, mix the sealer well and then apply it.

The leading edge's bladder twists and the valve goes into the leading edge

Remove the bladder for at least 50cm on each side thanks to the opening designed for that purpose. Put the seams of the bladder opposite those of the leading edge and put the bladder back in while keeping the seams opposite to each other.
Inflate the kite (without too much pressure) then tap the leading edge in order to help the bladder get back into its place. Inflate it completely and make a final check.
If it does not work, you will have to remove the leading edge bladder completely and replace it while taking care of keeping the right alignment.

A hole in the fabric

A sticker on each side will do if there are no shops close by. For a better quality repair, buy some Dacron sticker and round the angles. Stick a piece on each side of the hole. For holes or rips that are more than 5 cm wide, you must have your kite repaired. Many professionals offer such services: sail repair shops, shapers, shops and schools.

The footstraps are too big

If your feet are still loose even after you have adjusted your footstraps, you can put foam used for gym mats. Cut it in stripes as large as the footstraps and place them between the neopren and the Velcro band ®.

PRIORITY RULES

As on the road, the respect of a few priority rules makes it possible to ride without incidents. It's up to you to respect and inform the other riders of the following rules. The rider with the green kite has right of way.

- **The outgoing rider has right of way over the incoming rider**: the wind is often more turbulent on land than on the water. The rider who is on land is the one more at risk, which is why he has the priority.

- **When two riders converge**: the rider going starboard (kite right-hand side) has right of way and the rider going port tack (kite left-hand side) must give right of way and pass downwind with his kite as low as possible. There is no particular reason for this rule, but it is already applied in all other sports and nautical activities.

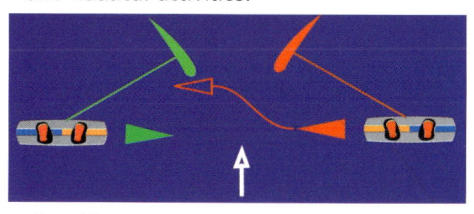

- **The rider going faster than another in the same direction must give way to the slowest rider**: the one going faster is the one who has a global vision of the situation since he arrives from behind.

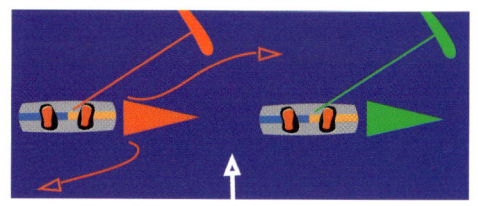

- **The rider passing upwind (windward) from another kiteboarder must fly his kite overhead**: the kiteboarder downwind (leeward) must fly his kite as low as possible.

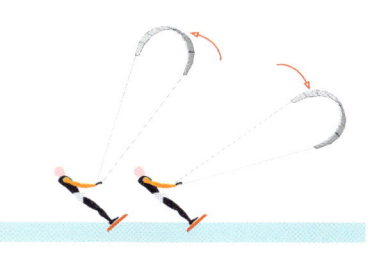

- **The rider surfing a wave has right of way over the one who is jumping or going in the opposite direction**: when surfing a wave, the kite is less easy to fly so there is less room for maneuvers. Nevertheless, the rule for the outgoing rider is applicable when the waves are close to the shore (shore break). In this case, the rider who is surfing will have to give way to the rider who is going out.

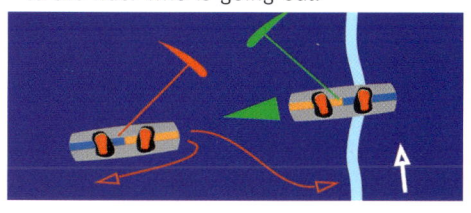

- **Right of way must be given to other ocean users**: kiteboarding is the latest nautical sport. It is not always well accepted and known by other ocean users. Kiteboard downwind to them.

- **A rider must have a clear safety zone of 50m downwind because he moves downwind when he jumps**: a rider must have a clear safety zone of 30m upwind to jump because the lines could touch the kite or the lines of another rider kiteboarding close by.

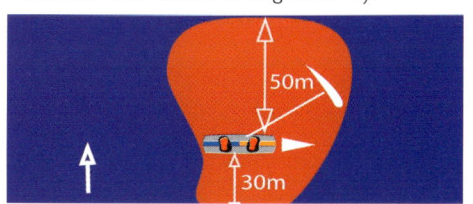

Practice

If the wind drops, place yourself "in" your kite and row with the board under your stomach.

Use the kite to come back to the shore after having wound the lines: go to the kite by winding the lines on the bar. Then, put the tip of the kite between your knees and follow the leading edge with your hands until you have reached the other tip of the kite.

Lie in the water and hold the kite by the tips, stretch as much as you can the arm that is in the air and bring the other arm under your body.

The wind suddenly picks up!

If the wind suddenly picks up, it's best to avoid coming back to the shore, expecting that someone will be there to help you because you might get seriously shaken on the beach.
The water being the safest place, come a bit closer to the shore but remain in the water and release your safety system (keep the kite leash connected).
This solution can result in getting the lines entangled but at least it is safe when you are overpowered.

In case of an extreme emergency, fly the kite directly towards the sea or the land and land it on its leading edge. If there is an obstacle in your path, the kite will meet it first and the traction will be lessened. Immediately release the bar and go to the kite. To secure the kite, deflate it or put weight on it (sand) and then disconnect the lines.

Running out of wind

If the wind suddenly drops, the first thing to do to protect yourself is wind the lines. Let go of the bar, but keep the kite leash connected. Once the kite is completely depowered (when it lays flat open like a flag), wind the lines and make sure that the kite remains depowered.

Winding the lines in the water

Bar with a re-ride system	Bar with a fixed leash
Pull on the leash until you have reached the bar	Pull on the leash until you reach the connection point of the leash on the lines
Wind the line that is connected to the leash starting from the bar	Keep the kite open and go to the bar. The line that is connected to the leash must be bent in two, starting from the point where the leash is connected to the lines
	Wind the lines of the folden leash starting from the bar (the kite must remain open). If it doesn't, it means that you are doing something wrong

For both systems

Wind all the lines until you have reached the kite

Make a knot to avoid the lines unwinding

Keep your kite inflated

Use your kite to drag you back to the shore by grabing both tips and lying on your board or letting it follow behind

Practice

All in good time! Work on your technique to land your jumps and try going higher for instance. Do it progressively in order not to get hurt.

If you are over confident, it will be easy for you to exceed your limits, and that is the moment you start being in danger. Be proactive: auto evaluation is better than waiting for an accident to happen!

When the kites tangle up

Someone else's kite could get entangled in your lines. When both kites are flying, it's dangerous. The lines can break because of the friction which results in the loss of control of the kite.
The pilot whose kite is entangled in the other person's lines must pull the release as quickly as possible. Careful, you must always have a kite leash. Releasing the safety without a leash could injure the other rider.

Then, both kites must be untangled. In order to do that, the rider whose kite is entangled in the other rider's line must disconnect his leash withoug letting it go, pass it through the other kite lines to untangle it and retrieve his leash. After that, the other kiteboarder can release his kite, and both of them can wind their lines.
If the rider who releases the kite does not have a leash, the rider who has not released first is in danger because he could be pulled with the power of two kites. In that case, the power loop and the leash must quickly be released.

A broken line

When a line breaks, what usually happens is that the kite goes into loops and generates power until it crashes.
This lasts a few seconds at most, and depending on which line breaks and the course of the rider, it can result in the kite crashing or the rider making a little jump first.
The only method to avoid breaking a line is to always check their state, not to have knots and to properly rinse and dry the equipment. Don't let cars roll on your lines and change them when they start wearing out.
If a line breaks while kiteboarding, do the same thing as when there is no wind (self rescue procedure). Release the bar, wind the lines and swim back to the shore or use the kite to pull you back.

If you are left-handed and that you ride on a twin tip, edge harder on your front leg to go to the right. With a directional board, edge harder on your back foot to go to the left. With practice and time, the feelings on both sides will become identical.

Tip: Riders that are more comfortable with their right foot forwards are called goofy; they are called regular if they are more comfortable with their left foot forwards.

TROUBLES AND REMEDIES

There is a twist in your lines

After a relaunch or a loop, there may be a twist in your lines. Do not worry, you can untwist them while kiteboarding. Here is how:

Untwist your lines when the kite is in the air
Put the kite at the top of the wind window. Put your bar above your head. Stretch your arms and twirl quickly.

Untwist the lines while kiteboarding
While kiteboarding, twirl the bar above the power loop (with a 4 line bar). Stretch your chest to avoid hitting your nose on the bar.
If you are flying a 2 line kite, stay hooked in the harness when you twirl the bar but be careful not to do it more than twice each time. Every time you untwist the lines, another twist is created in the harness line. With more than 2 twists, it will be impossible to unhook. Then unhook your harness line to undo the twist.

It is better to use a harness line connected to a swivel because you can untwist the lines as many times as you want.

Fear

Your mental state is as important as your physical state. If two riders of equal level take their time to go out when the conditions are rough (strong wind and waves, new spot) it is often in anticipation that one goes in the water first and watch him in action. This reaction is normal and it is caused by fear or apprehension. It's a good thing.

If you feel apprehension but manage it before kiteboarding, then all is well. But if a day comes when the weather conditions are too rough, and you can not control your fear, then it is best not to go out.

There is a limit to the degree of fear one can handle that must be respected. Loosing self control means loosing part of the pleasure, and being incapable of reacting properly, which increases the risk of accidents.

Fear is a natural protection that must be tamed. Your limits and your stress management will evolve with your practice level. It's up to you to find them.

Confidence also builds up with knowledge and that is another good reason to read this book!

Being over confident

You feel very powerful, nothing scares you, and you compare yourself to a professional. You try all the tricks and jumps and fall violently, but with an immense joy. You are probably in a phase where you are over confident.

It is usually at this moment that you can have an accident because pleasure has surpassed your conscious and you have stopped considering the risk factor. Don't forget that a professional who rides with a big kite in extreme conditions and who does spectacular jumps is trained and conscious of his own limits. If you try the things he does, your lack of experience will turn against you at one point or the other. Nothing replaces time and experience.

Practice

Going upwind is also called going leeward or close to the wind.

Principle

Going upwind is moving with an angle of 70° to maximum 45° in the direction from which the wind is blowing. This makes it possible to go from a point (A) to an upwind point (B) by tacking from one side to the next.

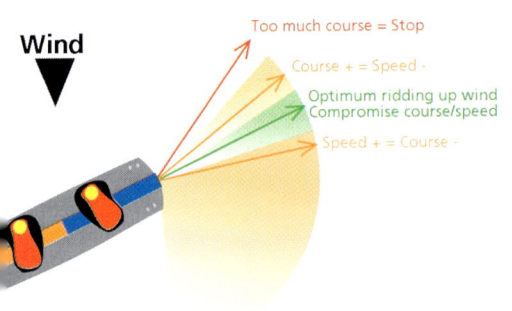

Wind

Too much course = Stop
Course + = Speed -
Optimum ridding up wind
Compromise course/speed
Speed + = Course -

Going upwind also allows you to come back to your starting point when there is a current or recover the distance you have lost after a jump.

To be able to go upwind, you must find a balance between the direction and the speed (green arrow).

Going too much upwind results in loosing speed and often coming to a stop (red arrow). Moreover, when you go too fast, apparent wind prevents you from going upwind (orange arrow speed + course -).

Practice will bring about the balance between the course (the direction in which you are moving) and the speed. When riding out to the sea, find a ship or a cloud that is further upwind and try to head for it. As you kiteboard towards the beach, choose a mark on the land (a tree or a house) and try to go upwind. Come back and look at your position according to your starting point.

In the best case scenario, the kite is placed at half of the wind window and you use the board to manage the power. To go upwind, you must maintain speed and have enough power to keep an edge. You speed up and slow down according to the changes in the wind speed, it is therefore important to react accordingly to continue to go upwind. The following examples describe what happens when we go upwind and don't anticipate the changes of wind speed.

Upwind cases

I go fast but I don't go upwind
There can be many reasons: the kite is too high up, you don't exert enough back foot and heel pressure to edge or you wait too long to edge heel side after the water start. Also, your kite might be too big and your board too large.

I go upwind and then stop
You are maybe edging too much heel side and are not releasing the edge when the wind or your speed decreases. You must put your board flatter on the water as soon as you feel your speed decrease and fly the kite up and down to regain speed.
If after having worked on this you still don't manage to regain speed, use a bigger kite or/and a bigger board.

I can go upwind on one side better than on the other
We all have a stronger side, so we must force ourselves to edge on the weak side more than on the other to obtain similar results on both sides. If you are right-handed and ride on a twin tip, edge harder on your front foot to go to the left.
With a directional board (more volume and bigger fins), edge harder on your back foot to go to the right.

MANAGING THE POWER

Managing the power is about coordination between piloting the kite and managing the stance on the board. It is not a matter of stopping but rather of being able to go slower or faster whenever necessary. The wind is rarely constant, so we must adapt to the conditions. It is the next step to your progression.

You can meet the following three cases:
1. The wind is rather stable and so is your cruising speed. Don't change a thing and mark the spot because the conditions are perfect!
2. The wind has increased and so has your speed. Move the kite closer to the water and exert heel side pressure to stabilize your speed. Careful though, edging too much heel side will make you loose speed completely. Keep the kite towards the sea until you feel that speed is manageable. Then put it at half height to be able to accelerate or slow down. You will have different feelings according to the water and wind conditions so it is normal that you perform better or worse accordingly. With a little practice, you will find the proper adjustment.
3. The wind has dropped and you have lost speed. Fly the kite to the top and don't exert too much heel side pressure, then fly the kite to the bottom again and slightly press heel side as the kite moves down. If you move the kite downwards without edging, you will loose part of the power because the board will skid.

GOING UPWIND

Whether you are learning or are having a hard time to go upwind, this chapter will help you!

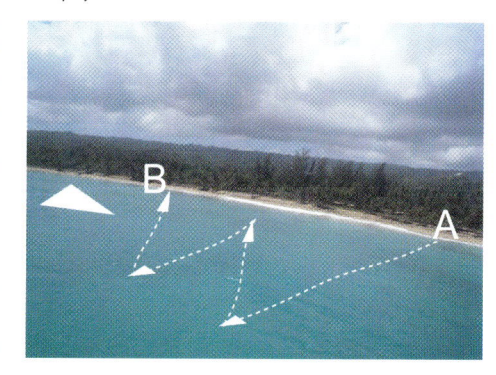

Practice

You will create a big spray but you will eventually stop. Once you know how to stop, all you need to do is anticipate and avoid gaining too much speed by not piloting the kite up and down. Instead, exert heel side pressure and put your body backwards once you feel that you have enough speed.
It will then be time to learn how to turn and go upwind.

More experienced riders can quickly slow down by going downwind and edging upwind immediately after. This technique puts the kite at the edge of the wind window and consequently, it pulls less.
Then, the rider must reposition himself above the board and exert toe side pressure until he draws a curve, then go downwind, quickly edge heel side and put his body backwards to increase the effect and create resistance against the kite.

In this case, the rider changes position according to the wind window.
In both cases, speed, and consequently the power of the kite, decrease.
Experience will teach you that the problem can be avoided by maintaining a constant edge right after the water start.

WWW.TAKOON.COM

Practice

You are in balance with power: your body is more stretched and your arms are slightly stretched to reduce the power (with a 4 line bar). Consequently, you ride more on your heel side.

2

Regain balance when the wind drops or when you fall backwards: fly the kite towards the top and pull on the bar to increase traction. At the same time, bend your legs (3a) and bring your chest forward so that your body doesn't act as a lever arm (3b) and it comes back over the board. Once balance is restored, go back to a stretched body position (2).

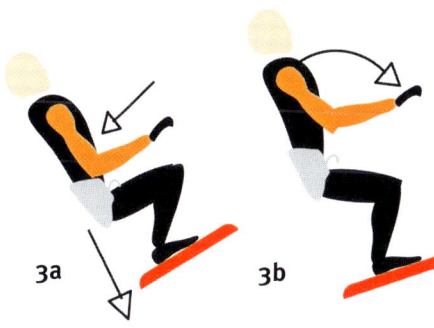

3a   **3b**

You are in balance with power but your position is wrong: your legs are stretched and you are pushing on your heels, but your chest is forward and your arms are stretched. Your lines are probably not adjusted properly (the trim system is not adjusted, or your back lines are too short). Another reason could be

4

that you do not dare putting your body backwards. Don't hesitate to stretch your body. It will help you manage your body, you will be more comfortable and avoid back pains.

You lose balance as you lose power: either you don't react, or you pull on the bar and move your hips forward. Managing your balance is thus harder and not effective. Try positions 3a and 3b.

5

SLOWING DOWN AND STOPPING

You are kiteboarding for the first time or for the first time with a lot of wind. You are gaining speed and as the board offers little resistance on the water, it is becoming more and more exhilarating. But as you are moving away from your starting point, you start to feel a little bit anxious and wonder... How do I stop?!

The first thing to do to slow down is to stop piloting the kite up and down and exert heel side pressure on you board while keeping your body stretched and leaning backwards (legs and chest). At the same time, push your bar (sheet out) to release the power from the kite.

Beware of the position of the kite in the wind window. If the kite is too high, you will not be able to maintain an edge. Put the kite at 11 or 1 o'clock, depending on which side you are going.

If you are still going fast after having stretched your body and taken as much an edge as possible, put a hand in the water (or even your bottom!) and put your kite to the top.

Practice

Toe side edging (2)

This position puts the board flat on the water. We use it to gain speed. With practice, you will be able to turn downwind.

Back foot pressure (3)

The effect of this stance depends on the type of board you are using.

On a twin tip

More weight on the back leg rather than the front reduces the surface of the board that is in contact with the water. More back foot pressure and heel side edging will help you control more power and ride upwind. Too much stance at the back reduces the power and prevents moving upwind.

On a directional

Back foot pressure is needed as most of the resistance to down wind drift comes from the fins rather than the edge of the board as with a twin tip. Less heel side pressure is needed because the fins create most of the traction.

Front foot pressure (4)

The front stance is very important to gain speed and to go upwind while combining it with heel side stance. It allows to maintain the longest possible surface of board in the water and to surf nicely when going upwind. This stance is therefore used when the wind is not strong, after the water start or to land jumps.

Combination of stance

To quickly change direction, combine a back stance with a toe side pressure (drawing 3+2).
To keep a course in light wind, use a heel and front stance.

Back stance combined with heel stance will help you start rotations during jumps or quickly slow down.

You will find more information on how to use the stances in the improvement chapter.

BALANCE

We know how to walk since our early childhood and we often play with balance.

To have balance on the water, we either need a big floating object, or work on what we call dynamic balance, meaning staying upright on a moving object. In our case, this object is a board and we go from an unstable position to a balanced one and coordinate it with the wind and the water.

For kiteboarding, the power of the kite intervenes and must be used to restore balance. The stances mentioned in the previous page are also very important. To manage your balance without hurting your back, you must also use your chest and bend your knees.

To learn how to have a good balance, you must look for the limits. You will have to fall in the water backward and forwards to find your marks and the right positions.

Manage your balance by working on these few positions.

You have balance with little power: your back leg is slightly more bent than your front leg, your arms are a little bent to be able to fly and you are leaning slightly heel side. Your hips, head and shoulders are turned in the direction of the travel.

1

After the water start

Water start is important. Once you stand on the board, you must keep your course and gain speed. This is usually not a problem.
Stay on your board, and fly your kite up and down, as close as possible to the water and then towards the top of the wind window. Remember that when you want to go to the right, you must fly the kite at the right of the wind window, and when you want to go to the left, you must fly it at the left of the wind window. When your speed is stable, you can work on your balance. Try leaning on your front leg, then on your back leg, then on your toes and heels. Bend your legs, and then stretch them. Try everything that is possible to record all the information on how the board and the kite respond, function, react, and interact.

THE STANCE

Before going any further, we must develop in more detail the notion of stance so that you can understand what moves to make in order to do what you want.

Direction and speed are managed by your kite and board.
The board reacts to your foot movement and what we call toe side or heel side edging.

Heel side edging (1)

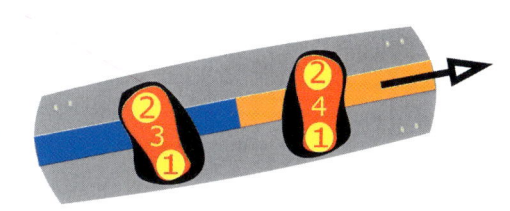

When you go upwind, the board has a big angle according to the surface of the water. It is the main kiteboarding stance. It makes you keep a course and ride into the wind direction (luff) by edging more.

Practice

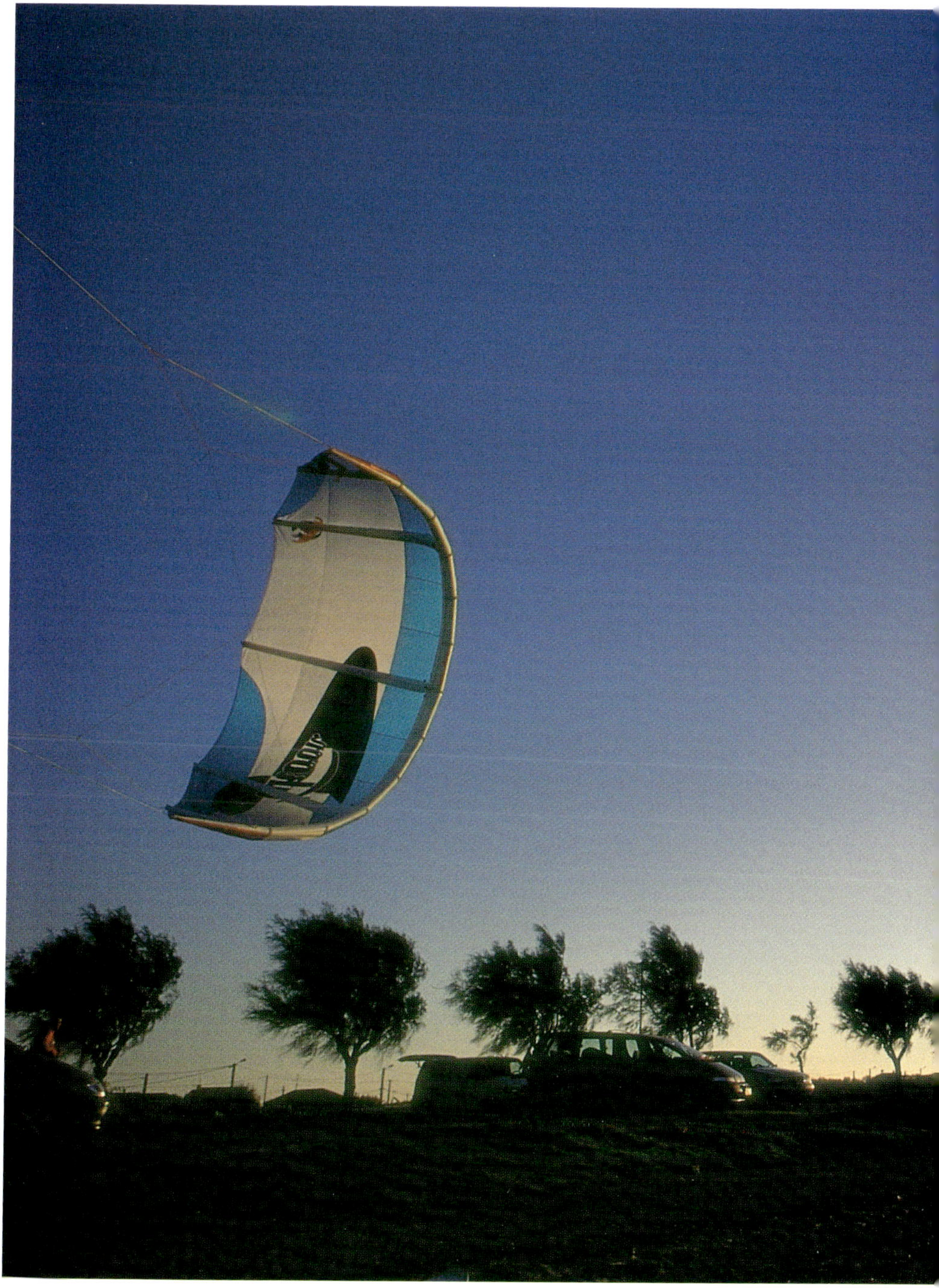

Practice

SOLUTIONS

Put your kite on one side of the wind window, it will be less affected by wind changes

Use a bigger kite, gradually increase the power, and measure the wind to realize what size kite to use in the future

Bend your legs and bring your shoulders towards your knees before flying the kite

Use at least a 175cm board and don't hesitate to use a board of 2 meters or more

You have a good balance but you must lean on the front foot and bring the back foot under your body while keeping the legs almost completely stretched.
Make sure you position your body above your board to gain speed

Unfold your legs sooner and lean on your heels

Look in front of you, towards the point you want to reach. Work on your heel side

Slightly stretch your front leg to move the board so that it is oriented more downwind

Bend your legs sooner and bring your chest closer to your body. If this doesn't work, use a bigger kite

Fly your kite lower, almost to the point where it touches the water, move it back up. Do it repeatedly

Bend your legs and keep them bent until you stand on the board

Fly the kite up and down to prevent it from falling and bend your legs.
This will enable you to regain balance

Fly the kite from top to bottom, and keep it on the side of the wind window that corresponds to your direction. If that doesn't work, use a bigger kite

Fly the kite higher in the wind window or use a smaller kite

You did it? Congratulations! You are now ready to check out the various possibilities that kiteboarding has to offer!

Water start reasons for failures

You can not stand on your board, or once you are on it, you fall... There can be numerous reasons why you can't make a water start. Check the following table to identify the case that corresponds to your problem and find its solution.

CASE	CAUSE
The situation, what you feel or observe	The cause can be due to a coordination, knowledge or positionning problem
The kite falls as you're getting ready for the water start	The wind may be unstable or you are skidding because of a current
	The kite is too small
You can not get up at all	Your legs are constantly stretched
	The board is too small
You get up but slide	You are probably using a twin tip or a board with too small fins
You get up but fall forwards	You bend your legs too much and your body can not counterbalance
	You look at your feet and edge too much toe side
	The board is not properly oriented
You fall backwards before gaining speed	You get up too late or the kite is too small
	You put the kite back to the top or too high in the wind window
	Your legs are too stretched out
	You pull on the bar and then release the tension. Careful, it doesn't work like a windsurf!
You fall backwards after having gained speed	You don't have enough power, you are putting too much pressure on the rail by pushing on your heels, or the board is too small
You are lifted above the board	The kite is too big or you are piloting too close to the water

Practice

Second scenario: the kite is on its leading edge
- Wait for the wind to blow in the kite.
- Pull on the bar as much as possible in order to reverse the angle of attack and let the kite fly backwards.
- Wait until the kite is in the air and then release tension on one side of the bar. The kite is then going to turn.
- Push the bar away from you when the kite can fly to the edge of the wind window.

Arc valved foil kites and inflatable kites can be relaunched the same way.

THE WATER START

Getting ready for the water start

To learn how to water start, you must know how to fly a kite from one side of the wind window to the other without making it fall. You must know how to relaunch a kite from the water, fly with one hand in order to recover your board with the other hand and with the help of the board leash, use the safety systems and put your feet into the footstraps. You can use the footstraps to place the board in the proper direction. Always keep an eye on the kite though! Put your hands at the center of the bar to avoid piloting errors and put the kite slightly to the left or right at the top of the wind window for it to be more stable.
Then train to body drag with your feet in the foot straps.

The principle

There are a few discovery steps you must go through before finding the right body position and associating it to the kite piloting.
The water start principle is to use the power of the kite to lift you up on the board and then gain speed. It is an important step. There are exercises you can do with the help and advice of your instructor.

1. Positionning your body:
Legs must be bent for the body to be as close as possible to the board. When you fly the kite for the water start, your shoulders must move towards your knees until the traction created by the kite pulls you up on your board. All you need to do then is stay up on the board.
To gain speed, always put pressure on the front foot.

2. Piloting the kite:
Start with the kite at the top. You must then fly the kite in the opposite direction from the one you wish to ride and make it pass in the wind window to achieve the necessary power to be pulled on your board. Always start at the top of the wind window, and then make trials by positioning the kite lower and lower, until you have the necessary power.

Practice

4. The kite moves to the edge of the wind window. Pull on the side of the kite that is in the air. If the kite is still moving to the top, continue, it will launch. If the leading edge moves towards the sea, it means that the kite does not have the right angle according to the wind. Wait before trying again.

Relaunching a 4 line inflatable kite:
1. The kite is laying on its leading edge. Wait until the kite lines have tension and most importantly, don't change your hands side on the bar. It is normal that the lines have crossed because the kite has made half a turn.
2. Release the power of the kite as much as possible, by pulling on the power strap and pushing the bar as much as possible.
3. Swim towards the kite. It must flip. If it doesn't, you can pull the center line (make sure that the lines are not tangled). This will help the kite flip over.
4. As soon as you see what side the kite is moving to, swim in the opposite direction, until one tip is close to the sea and the other towards the sky. Pulling on the center line will help move the kite to the edge of the wind window.
5. Pull on the line that is close to the water and let go of the other side.
6. The kite moves towards the edge of the wind window. Pull on the side of the kite that is in the air. If the kite moves to the top, continue, it is going to launch. If the leading edge moves towards the water, the kite does not have the right angle according to the wind. Wait before trying again.

Relaunch a valved foil kite

First scenario: the kite is on its trailing edge
- Check for obstacles downwind because the kite can pull you for a dozen of meters. If the wind is onshore, and you are close to the shore or close to an obstacle, use your safety system and return to the land before relaunching.
- Use the power strap to reduce the power.
- Push the bar away from your body as much as possible to reduce the power even more.
- Air goes in the kite and it launches.

and briefly explain the key points to your assistant. Show him the leading edge and describe it "the big tube that goes from one tip of the kite to the next". Tell him that you will fly the kite close to the shore and that he will have to move towards the kite and firmly grab the big tube. Make sure to tell him not to let it go until you have recovered it.

The moment your assistant grabs the kite, walk towards him to release the tension in the lines and kill the power of the kite. Then recover it. Don't forget to unhook from your harness but keep the kite leash connected.

With a foil kite:
The principle is the same whether you use an arc kite or a flat kite. Explain the procedure mentioned above to your assistant but instead of grabbing the leading edge, ask him to grab one of the tips. Tell him that once he has grabbed it, the kite is going to flap and that it is normal. Land and quickly recover your kite.

Landing alone

Whether there is no one left on the beach or you are kiteboarding alone, you will still have to land. The easiest way to land your kite on your own is to use your safety system, which by the way is a good way to practice. Your kite leash must absolutely be connected.

Put your kite at the top of the wind window and let go of the bar. Walk downwind towards the kite as it lands. This will reduce the speed of its fall. If you go upwind as it goes down, it will increase the speed of the fall.

If you let go of the bar when the kite is at the edge of the wind window, it will roll downwind and could get damaged.

This procedure can be done in the water as well if the ground surface might damage the kite.

Once you have landed the kite, walk to it by keeping tension on the line connected to the leash. That is the only line that you can grab. Grabbing another one is dangerous because the kite could regain tension and power up again.

LAUNCHING THE KITE FROM THE WATER

It's inevitable. At one point, you will have to relaunch the kite from the water, whether you are learning in a school, you have chosen to use a high performant kite, or you want to try new tricks.

Relaunching a 2 line inflatable kite:
1. The kite is on its leading edge. Wait for the lines to regain tension and don't change your hand's sides on the bar. It is normal that the lines are crossed because the kite has made half a turn.
2. Bend your arms, swim towards your kite and at the same time, stretch your arms. The kite must flip on its top skin.
3. Once the kite is positioned with one of its tips close to the water and the other in the air towards the sky, pull on the line that is in the water and release the opposite side. If the kite moves to the right, swim a little to the left to help it launch. Swim to the right if the kite moves to the left.

Practice

Piloting problems related to the bar

My kite does not turn properly

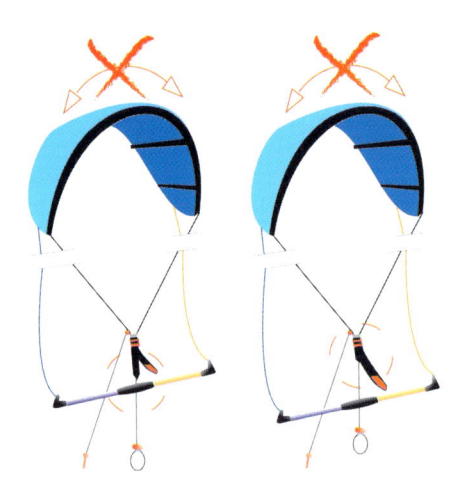

Your bar is too small or the front lines are too short. Try to lengthen the power strap on the front lines, pull the bar to you (sheet in) or use a bigger bar. The kite must react as soon as you put pressure on either side of the bar.

My kite moves backwards when I launch or when the wind is not strong

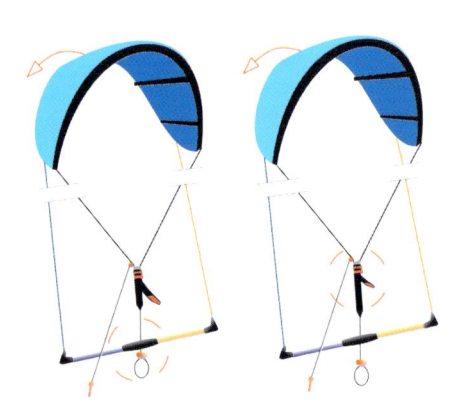

You pull too much on the bar or the front line power strap is too long. Therefore, the angle of attack of the kite reverses or is too big. Pulling on the bar is useless. Shorten the length of the power strap or pull less on the bar.

The kite is not stable at the top
Sheet in a little: use the trim system to add length to the front lines. If regardless of this the kite is still unstable at the top, make sure the problem is not caused by unstable wind. If the wind is not the source of the problem, and that the kite has a high aspect ratio, avoid putting it at the top.

LANDING THE KITE

Landing with an assistant

You want to land, so your assistant moves towards your kite and grabs it. Piece of cake! It is easy for a kiteboarder to help you, but it is less obvious for an inexperienced person. Regardless of his good will to help, he might let go of your kite after grabbing it or grab it by the trailing edge. Whether you have a foil or an inflatable kite, take time to explain to the person who is going to help you how to proceed and make sure he or she has understood.

With an inflatable kite:
Put your kite at the top of the wind window

Self Launching (without help)

Wear your harness, helmet and flotation vest before getting ready to launch.

Hold the kite by one of the tips. Put it on the ground according to the angle it will take while in the air. Fold the tip and cover it with sand or with a sandbag.

Reduce the kite power with the power trim, connect the kite leash but don't hook into the harness. Position yourself in the axe of your kite (in the same direction than the imaginary line that links both tips). If the kite topples to the front, you are too much upwind. If it topples to the back, you are too much downwind.

Launching a foil kite:
The rigging procedure is the same than with an inflatable kite. The foil kite must be pre-inflated. It is then launched with a little bit more power than for an inflatable kite. Position yourself in order to have a 45° angle between your lines and the wind.

Once the kite is in the air, adjust the power with the power strap.

Practice

Tip to never make a mistake while connecting a 4 line kite

Some brands use different knots on the front and back lines: a larkshead knot for the front lines and a figure 8 knot for the back ones for example. This method avoids making mistakes such as connecting a front line instead of a back line. It is advised to use this method as you will immediately know if you have made a mistake or not.

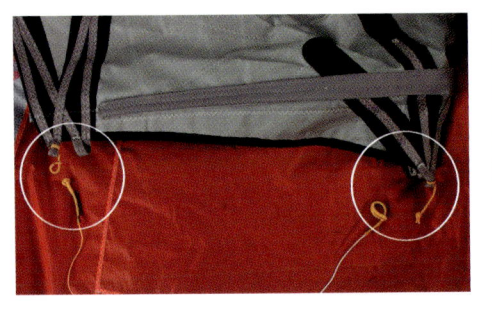

The following picture shows the connection knots for the front (right) and back (left) lines.

Launching the kite

Wear your harness, helmet and flotation vest before getting ready to launch. Regardless of the type of kite you use, your bar must be equipped with a functional safety system and you must learn how to use it before flying the kite. Always simulate triggering your safety system before launching your kite, put your hand on the safety release while launching and be ready to trigger it if necessary.

Launching with an (unknown) assistant
Position the lines 90° to the wind. Ask your assistant to firmly hold the kite's leading edge in front of him, not to move and let the kite go only once you have given him a specific signal (thumb up). Ask him to repeat the information. Get ready, put tension in the lines, and then move upwind until the kite stops flapping. Then signal your assistant and slowly fly the kite.

Rigging a 4 lines kite, bar upwind

1. Unwind the lines, starting from the kite and going upwind. Put the right side of the bar on the right side of the kite. Place your legs as shown on the picture.
2. Unwind the lines starting from the bar. Put the front lines (middle lines) between your legs, the back lines (the ones on the side) on each side of your body and walk to the end of the lines.
3. The lines are unwound.
4. Lay the lines on the ground while keeping the back lines on the side and the front lines in the middle.
5. Put the kite on the front lines and connect the front lines to the leading edge (the side of the kite that is lying on the ground).
6. Connect the back lines to the trailing edge (the tip of the kite that is in the air).
7. Check the lines by walking to the kite while holding the back lines. Once you have reached the kite, you must be holding the lines that are at the exterior of the kite and that are connected to the trailing edge.
8. Position the line 90º to the wind. Preferably launch with an assistant, and check that the lines are connected properly by outstretching the front lines from the bar before confirming the launch.

Once ready and sure that the lines are properly connected, connect yourself to the bar.

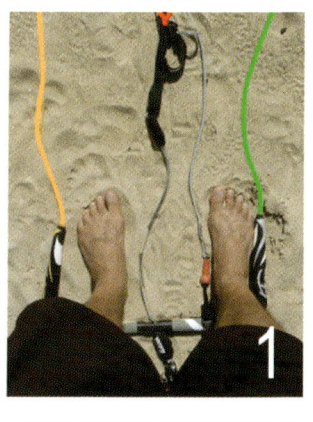

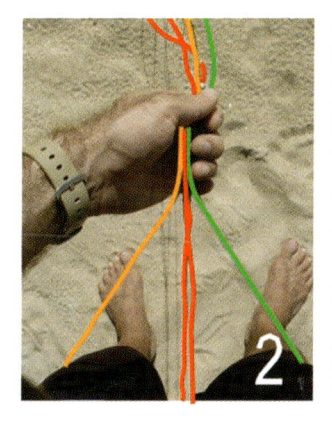

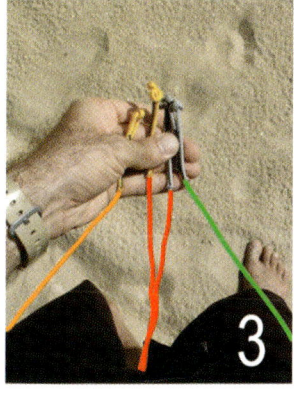

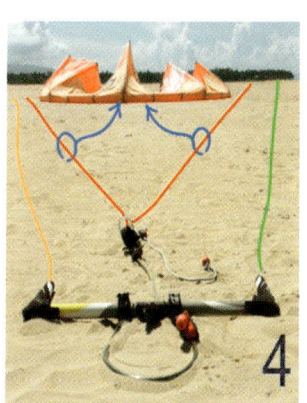

Practice

To easily unwind the lines, put the front lines (the ones that meet at the center of the bar) between your legs and the back lines (the ones that are at the extremities of the bar) on each side of your body (see picture).
Unwind the lines from the bar starting from the kite and going downwind.

1. Put the bar upside down (the right to the left) for it to be on the right side according to the kite. Put a feet on each side of the central line.
2. Unwind the lines starting from the bar. Put the front lines between your legs, a back line on each side of your body, and walk to the end of the lines.
3. The front lines are still between your legs and the back lines on each side.
4. Lay the front lines on the ground and the back lines on each side of the kite. Make sure you leave space between the lines. Connect the front lines (the ones that are in the middle) on the side of the kite that is lying on the ground (the leading edge).
5. Connect the back lines (the ones that are on the side) on the side of the kite that is not in contact with the ground (the trailing edge).
6. Make sure that the lines are properly connected by lifting the side lines from the bar (they must be parallel and not crossed with any other line).

This is called a preflight check. Always do one before launching your kite.

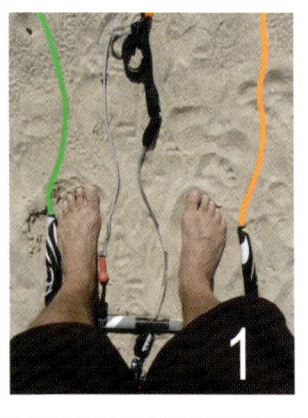

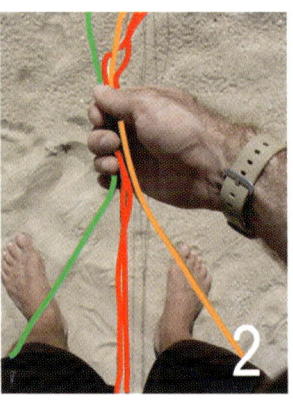

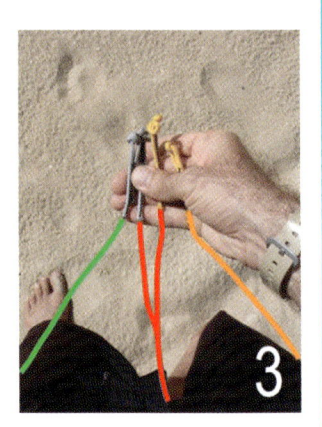

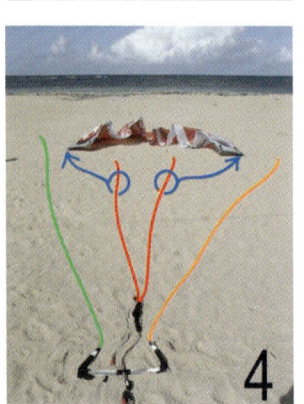

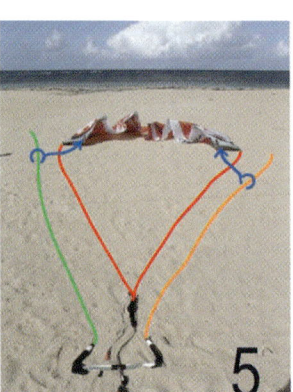

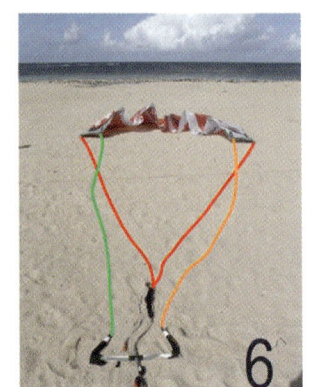

RIGGING AND LAUNCHING

Rigging a 2 line inflatable kite

Unwind the lines, check the bridals and make sure that there are no knots: you must be able to make out a rectangle when you take the pig tail knots in one hand and the knots of the back bridal in the other. Connect the lines to the kite.

Rigging a 4 line kite with the bar downwind

This technique is preferred than the following one because it allows to check that the lines are properly set. Having the kite positioned upwind also avoids involuntary launches.

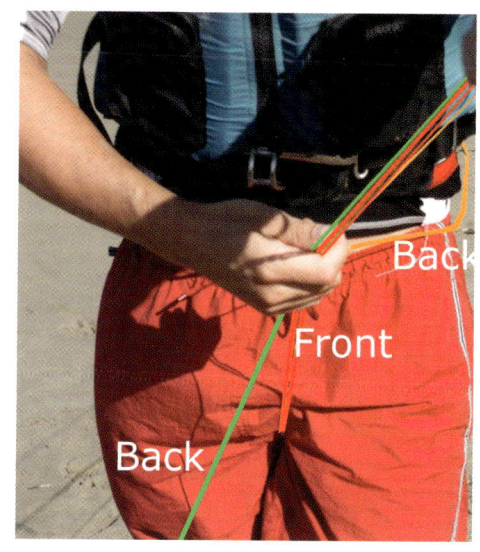

Practice

Positioning yourself according to the wind:
If you don't know whether an obstacle influences the wind or not and you wish to kiteboard, observe the spot carefully before launching. The birds may have a hard time to fly, the flags may be flapping and then not moving. These are all signs that you are in a zone where the wind is unstable.

Put your kite at half of the wind window. This will prevent you from loosing control or being unvoluntarily lifted.

The average distance of the turbulence downwind is approximately 7 times longer than the height of the buildings or obstacles that created it. It increases or decreases according to the speed of the wind.

The following formula calculates the length of the turbulence:
L = S x H/2
L: the length of the turbulence in meters
S: the speed of the wind in meters per second
H: the height of the obstacles in meters

Here's an example: a 30 meter high building is upwind. The wind blows at 3 Beaufort, in other words 4.5 m/s.
The formula shows the following result:
4.5 x 30/2 = 67.5
There will be turbulences for 67.5 meters at ground level.

If the wind blows at 7 Beaufort, in other words 14m/s, the turbulence will be of 210 meters at ground level (14 x 30/2 = 210).

To conclude, the obstacles create greater turbulence the stronger the wind. We must therefore be more careful and move downwind.

Don't launch or land behind trees and buildings and don't kiteboard in front of obstacles. You might get lifted and seriously injured.

The bay effect

When there are big obstacles along the shore of a bay, the wind changes direction accordingly. It is often the case close to headlands going into the sea, cliffs or mountains. You can also notice that the wind speed increases (at the right bottom of the picture).

The Venturi effect

The Venturi effect is present almost everywhere there is an obstacle, but we feel it when it is created by big shapes like hills, sand dunes, trees, or buildings. The wind has suddenly less space to travel in, so it must accelerate between the obstacles and regain its initial speed after.

The main danger is the wind acceleration. If it is not anticipated, you can be overpowered and loose control as you reach the affected zone. On the other hand, and with light winds, the Venturi effect makes it possible for you to kiteboard.

Don't over exaggerate the risks, a few small trees or houses are not going to endanger your riding. You must know how to make the difference, but never neglect high obstacles (10 meters and above).

When the wind comes from the sea, it pushes you directly onto the beach. Make sure that you have enough space downwind on the shore to release the kite without danger and that there is at least 100 meters between you and obstacles.

Observing the wind force to choose the kite size

Take your time to find out what the wind force is by using an anemometer or by observing the external signs such as the water condition or the way the trees bend. Use a smaller kite size than the one used by the good local rider, or if you are not sure what size to choose, start by rigging a smaller kite even if you later change for a bigger one. Time will teach you what kite size to choose with one look.

Whatever the case, when you launch your kite, don't put it at the top of the wind window until you are sure the wind is stable and that you don't have too much power in the kite. You will always be safe that way because the wind can not lift you, it can only pull you.

If you are pulled even though your kite is at the edge of the wind window, it means that you have chosen a kite that is too big. Land or use the safety system and rig a smaller one.

If you feel jolts in the bar, or see your kite going backwards and forwards, it means that the wind is unstable. In that case, land your kite.

Dangers and wind effects

There are various wind effects. For safety reasons, beginners and advanced kiteboarders must understand them to know how to position themselves in order to avoid dangers while launching, landing and practicing.
Obstacles can change the direction of the wind. The stronger the wind, the more the turbulences are big and dangerous.

Whirlwinds

Obstacles alter the wind direction. When the change of wind direction created by the obstacles is quick, it creates turbulences that make piloting difficult and even dangerous, as the kite could get caught in the whirlwind.

Whirlwind downwind from the obstacle can lift a kiteboarder up and drop him as suddenly. All kiteboarders must be aware of this effect. The speed of the wind determines the zone in which the kite will be affected.

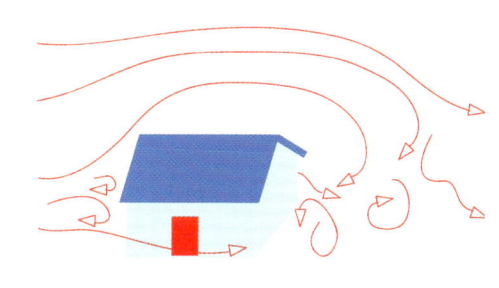

The buildings of a city, a forest or a cliff create whirlwinds when the wind is sideshore or side-on-shore. This is dangerous for launching. To avoid the wind turbulences, launch the kite sea side and at the edge of the wind window, and keep it close to the ground or the water surface until you are in the water. When a kite is at the top, it is more sensitive to the turbulences.

Practice

are reserved to beginners and check the local rules. Consult the local riders and if there is a kiteboarding or sailing school close by, ask for information there.

Choosing your location

Observe the environment: it is the first thing to do before deciding to go riding or not.
The water: check that the sea bottom is not dangerous (rocks, reefs, oyster beds, boat wrecks are all potential hazards).
The ground: make sure that there is enough distance downwind in order not to get hurt in case of a piloting mistake. Kiteboarding before cars, houses, rocks is not safe.

Estimate the length of the beach to assess whether or not you will be able to come back to the shore if you can't ride upwind.

Others: avoid crowded spots. It is best to ride downwind from other beach users. All this is called making a navigation plan, but before knowing whether or not you have chosen the right spot, you must check that the wind is ok for kiteboarding.

Observing the wind orientation
Kiteboard with the following wind orientations: Side-shore (parallel to the beach) and side-on-shore (slightly from the sea). Make sure there is a withdrawal point downwind in case of a problem.

The safest condition to kiteboard is with side shore wind (drawing above).

In any case, stay clear from obstacles.

Don't kite when the wind comes from the land (off-shore wind).

Don't kite when the wind comes from the sea (on-shore wind).

GETTING READY

Taking charge of the equipment

After having learnt in a school, take time to get familiar with the new equipment you are going to use. Adjust the footstraps of your board and make sure your bar is properly set.

Adjusting a 4 line bar
Most of the new bars sold on the market are set and can be connected without having to make any preliminary adjustments on your kite. Yet if you buy a second hand bar, or your bar is new and the lines have to be adjusted, or a line breaks and you have to change it, you will have to fix your bar on your own so that your lines are at equal length and your bar is placed at the right distance from your body.

Here are the steps to perfectly adjust your bar: Tie the lines to a fixed point (a hook or a nail for instance).

1. **The front lines:** first check their length without putting any tension in the lines. The lines must draw a curve, so that is it easy to see which one is longer. Once the lines are of the same length without tension, firmly pull on them to check the length once again.
2. **The back lines:** stretch your arms and pull on the bar to check the length of the lines that are on each side of the bar (the back lines). If your bar is not perpendicular to the front lines when you pull on the back lines, use the knots on the leader lines to adjust them.
3. **The general adjustment:** adjust the power strap of the front lines at half of its length. Connect the front lines to your harness, step back to create tension in the lines, then pull on the bar to stretch the back lines. If the bar is too close to your body, shorten the back lines at equal length by using the leader lines. If your arms are too stretched out, add length to the back lines or shorten the front lines.

The goal is to have a comfortable cruising position and the ability to control the power of the kite. When the lines are tensed, the bar must be at 20 centimeters from your body.

Advice: remove the harness line if you do not use it for jumping.
For safety reasons, always try a new bar with light wind. You will become familiar with the way it controls the kite, and most importantly, you will realize if there are any problems in the line adjustments.

Ajusting a 2 line bar
All that needs to be done is to stretch and tie the lines. Adjust them at equal distance by moving the knots on the leader lines and then place the harness line in the center. Avoid putting it too much in the middle because it will impair the bar. Make sure the leash is long enough so that you can grab your board.

From a technical view point, you are set, so let's move to the practice area.

Access to the beach

Access to the beach is either public or private. It depends on the various regulations in different countries. Find out where the authorized spots are, the places reserved to kiteboarding, and the water access. Don't kiteboard in areas that

Practice

THE COMPASS ROSE

The compass rose describes the possible courses a kiteboarder can take according to the wind. These courses vary according to the performance of the kite, the board and the pilot. It is impossible to go directly downwind with a kite in normal wind and navigation conditions.

The sailing points are determined according to the wind and not according to the land because the various possible courses are induced by the wind direction.
For instance, when we move perpendicular to the wind, it is called going cross to the wind.

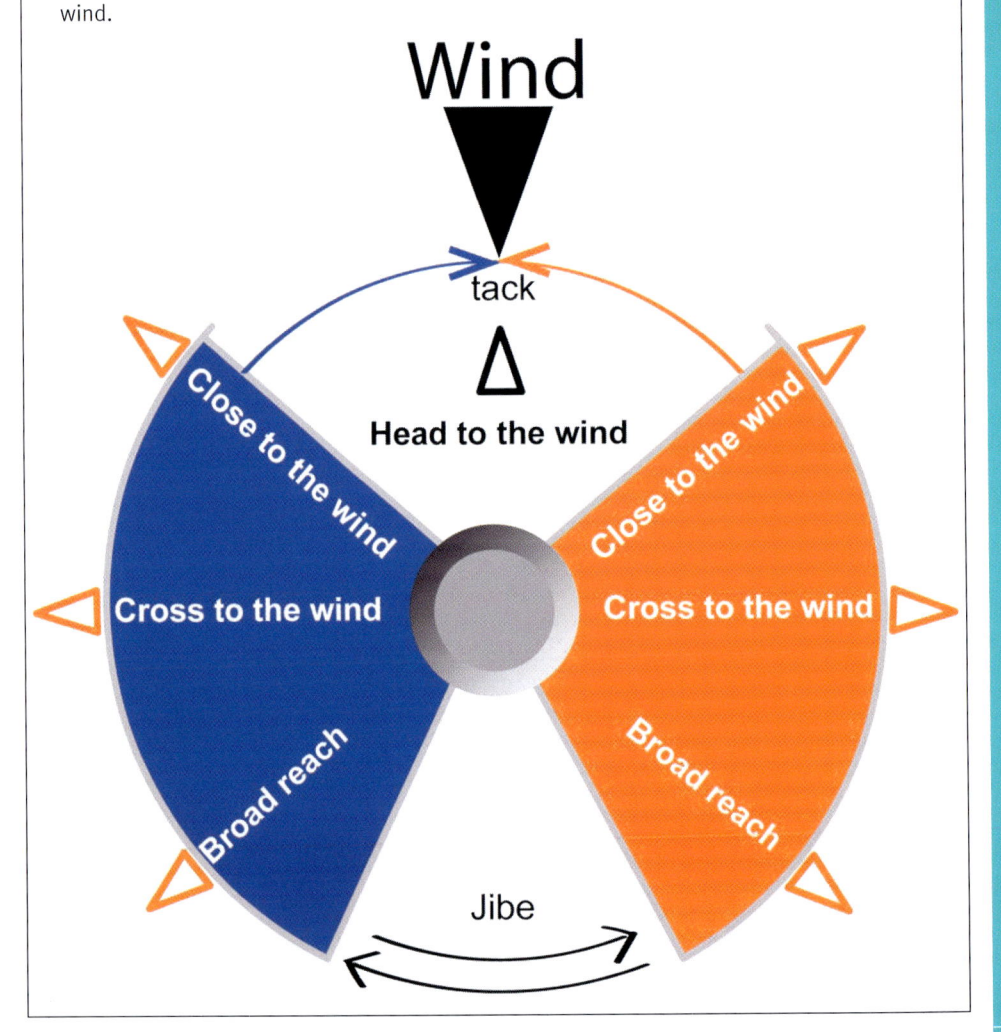

Wind

tack

Head to the wind

Close to the wind

Close to the wind

Cross to the wind

Cross to the wind

Broad reach

Broad reach

Jibe

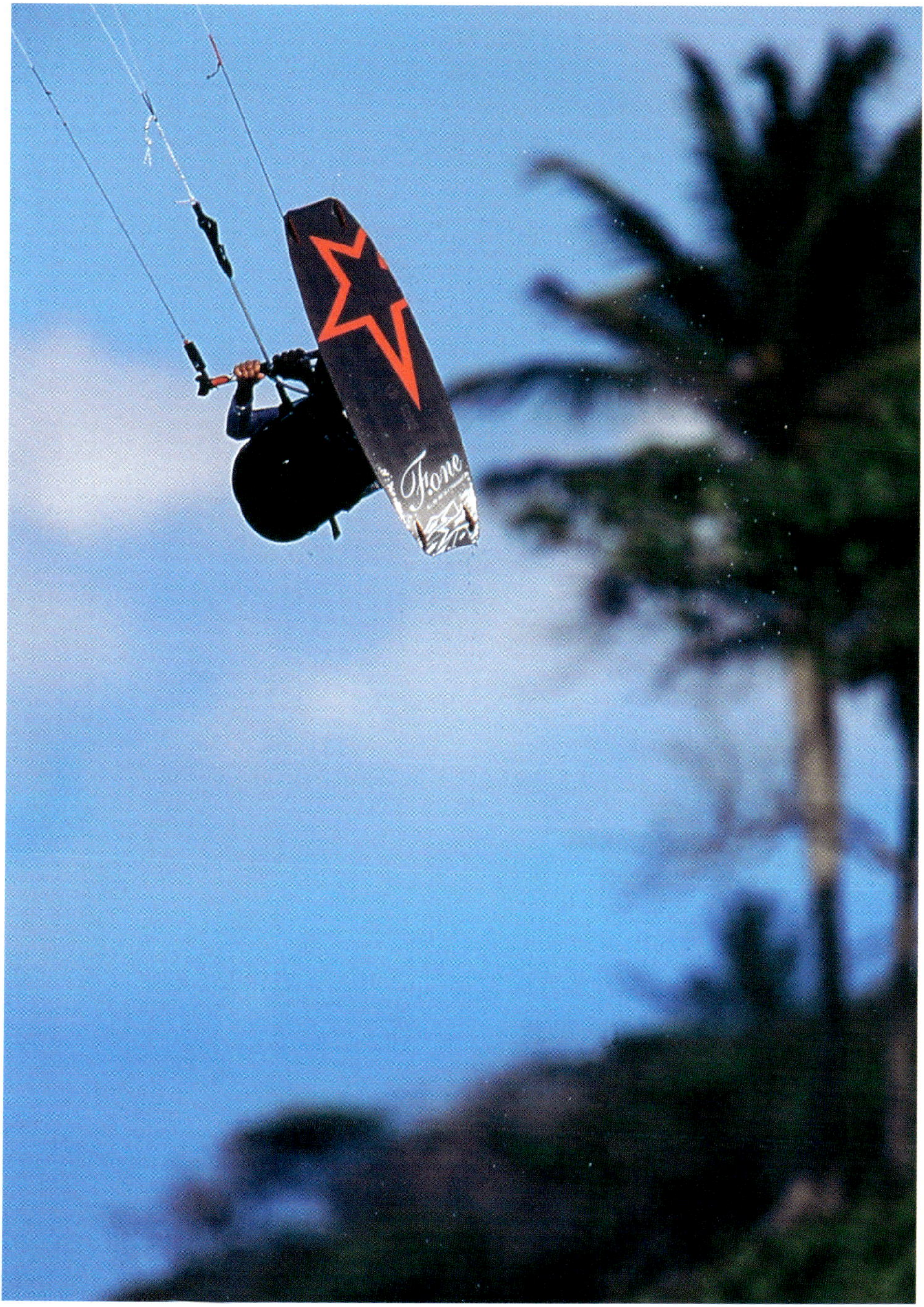
F.one

Practice

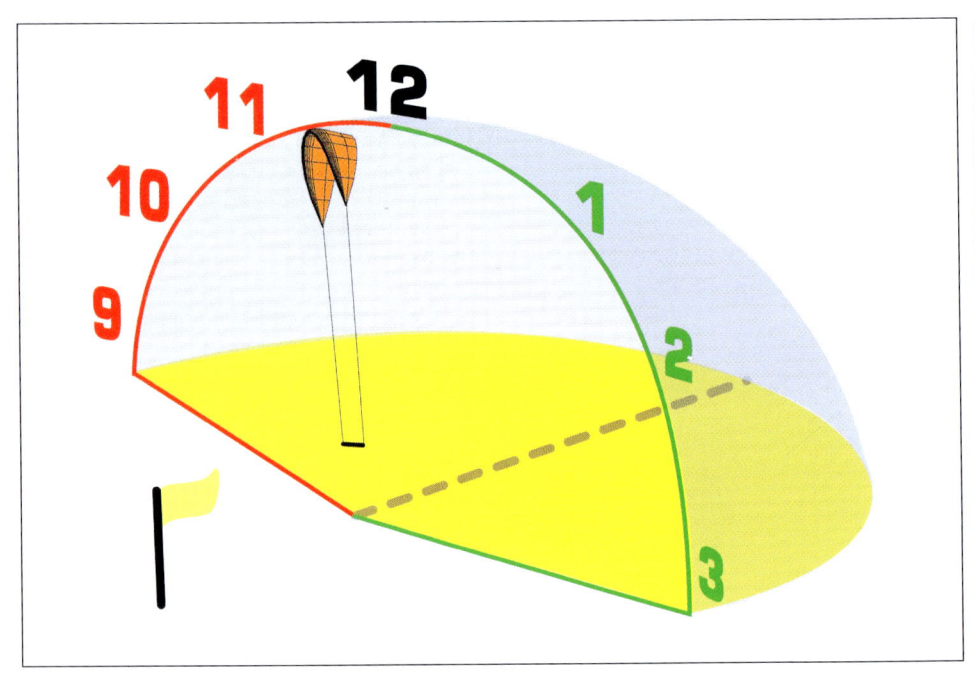

- **A** Top or zenith
- **B** Neutral zone
- **C** Power zone
- **D** Launching & landing

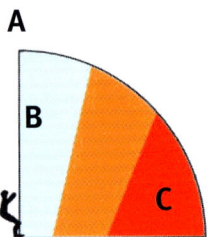

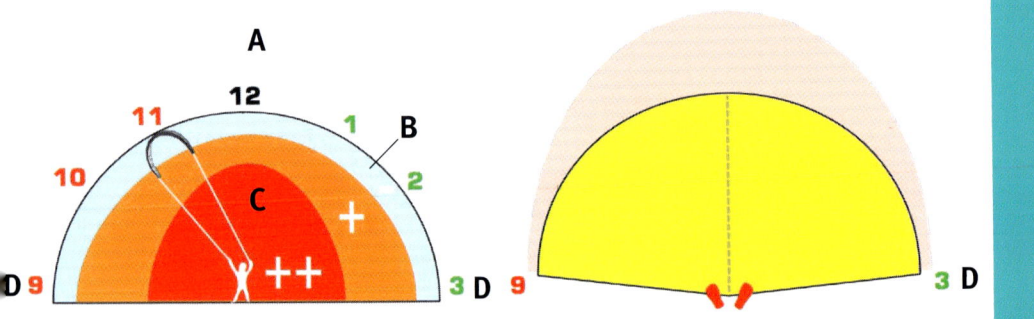

DIRECTIONS

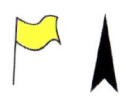

The arrow illustrates the wind seen from above, the flag describes the wind seen from the side or in 3D.

The red shapes illustrate what the position of the feet should be.

The arrows on the feet illustrate the movement that the feet or any other body part should do.

The yellow dots illustrate the points you must put pressure on to have an effect on the board.

The big arrows illustrate the path that must be followed.

The wind windows illustrate the position of the kite at the various moments of a manoeuvre or a jump.

NAVIGATION TERMINOLOGY

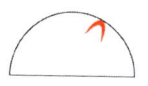

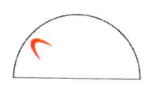

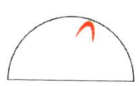

"Are you ready to kiteboard? Ok, first go straight, and then port side!"
"All right, but... what is port side?!"
To avoid this kind of embarrassment, here are a few technical navigation terms.

Starboard: *to the right.*
Port side: *to the left.*
Starboard: *kiteboarding with the kite to your right, thus towards your right.*
Port side: *kiteboarding with the kite to your left, thus towards your left.*
Upwind: *we are upwind from someone or something when the wind hits us before the person or object.*

Downwind: *we are downwind from someone or something when the wind hits the person or the object before us.*
To luff: *the act of sailing closer to the wind (changing direction towards the wind).*
Bear away: *change direction downwind.*
Course: *a direction.*
Edging: *the action of pressing hard on the board with the heels.*
Sailing points: *the direction according to the wind.*
Ride: *kiteboarding in a direction.*
For instance, we say ride upwind, cross wind, broad-reach run. The compass rose illustrates this better.

THE WIND WINDOW

The wind window represents a quarter of a sphere, centered on the pilot, and describes the area in which the kite flies. Yet its size varies according to the size of the lines and the performance of the kite that is used, which influences the angle to the right and left of the pilot.
When you fly the kite to the right, you are pulled to the right (green side). When you fly the kite to the left, you are pulled to the left (red side).

Technical terminology of the wind window
The top: the easiest position to fly without power.
Edge of the wind window: if you fly slowly, it is the trajectory in which your kite flies. It is at the limit of the wind window, the less powerful zone.
Power zone: it is the place where the kite gets the most power. It is used for body dragging, water start and jumps.

Understanding the power zones gives you visual marks and knowledge as to where to position your kite and how to anticipate its reactions. These marks will be useful throughout your progression.

Practice

Directions
Navigation terminology
The wind window
The compass rose
Getting ready
Rigging and launching
Landing the kite
Launching the kite from the water
The water start
The stance
Balance
Slowing down and stopping
Managing the power
Going upwind
Troubles and remedies
Priority rules
Equipment tips

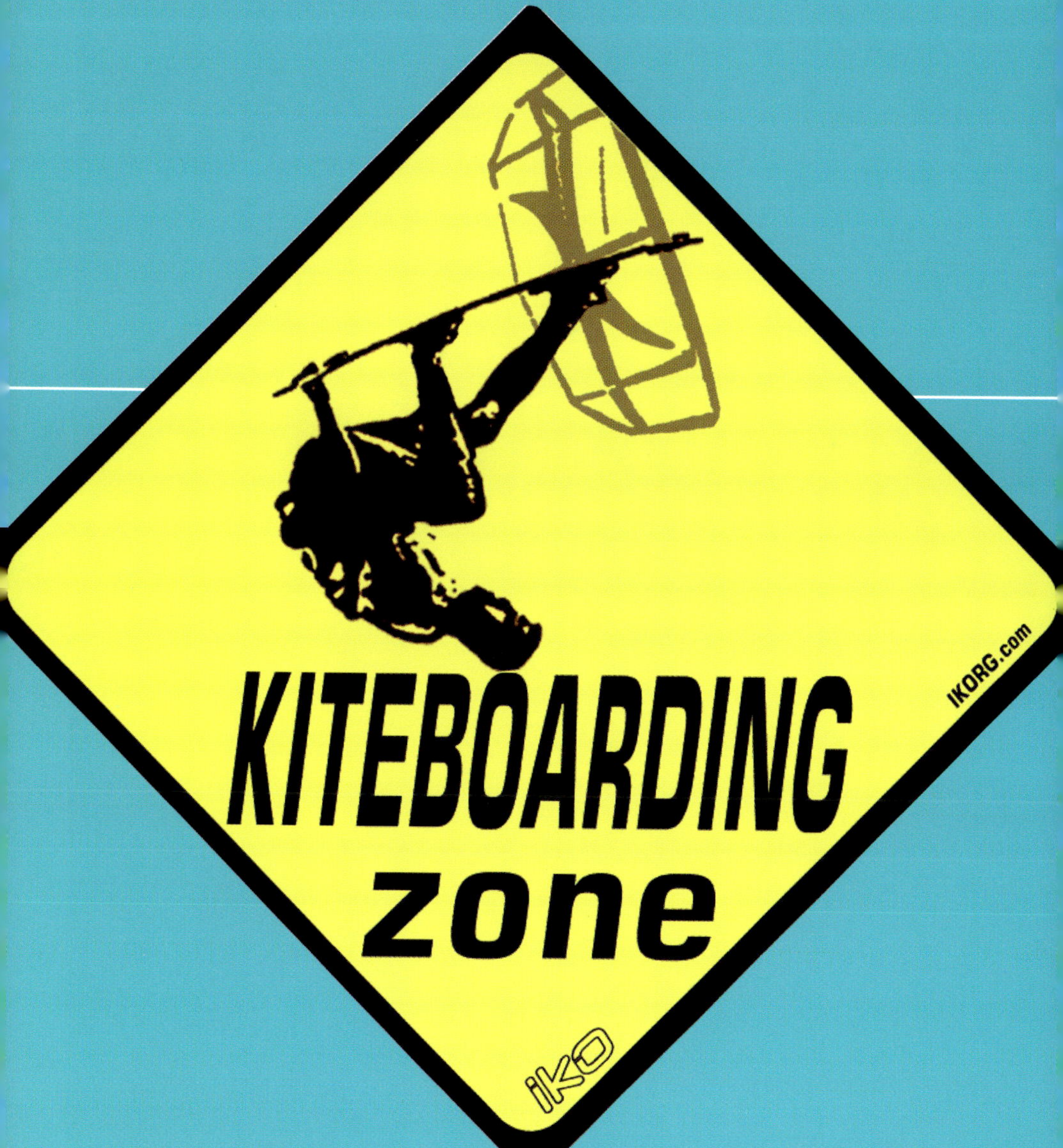
KITEBOARDING
zone
IKORG.com
iKO

The helmet

The main purpose of the helmet is to avoid injuries that can be caused by the board (when it is connected with a leash), but also to protect from impact while learning how to jump and during launching and landing. It must be water resistant, not obstruct your hearing faculty nor obstruct your sight. It is recommended to constantly wear one regardless of your level. No one is completely safe from harm. Stylish helmets that have an internal protection of less than two centimeters do not protect you in case of severe impact!

The impact vest

This vest is used by wakeboarders. It is covered by an absorbing skin that diminishes the effect of the impact on the water in case of a rough fall.

Complementary equipment

Every place has its specificities: Australians will make sure to never forget their sun block cream and their hats, Europeans will always wear a neoprene suit, in the Reunion, they will always wear booties to be able to walk on the reef or avoid sea urchins. It's up to you to adapt your equipment according to where you are to be comfortable and secure.

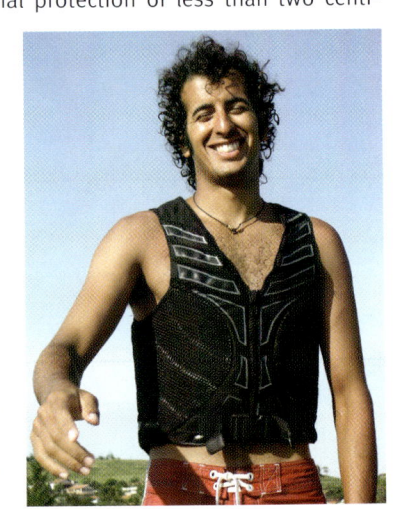

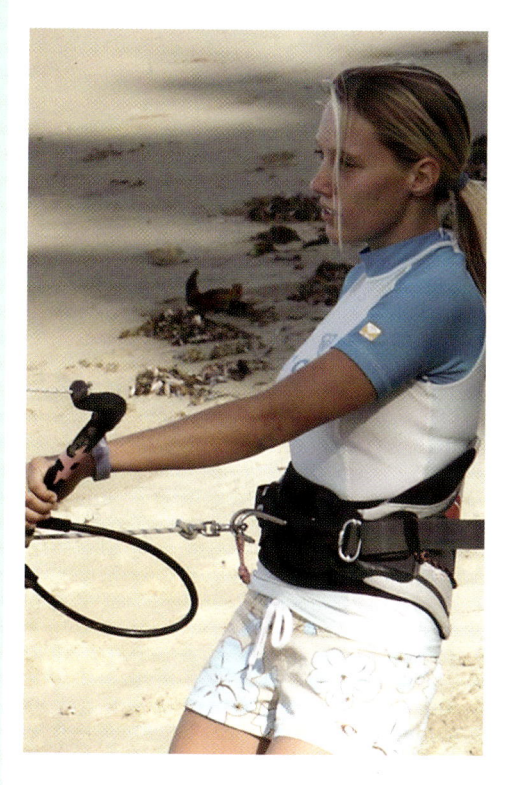

THE RIDER'S EQUIPMENT

The harness

The seat harness
Kiteboarding with a seat harness is comfortable and avoids many unecessary efforts. Because the harness buckle is lower than on a waist harness, you must put a long harness line to have a comfortable position when you are hooked in.
If the seat harness is not specifically designed for kiteboarding, the spreader (harness bar) will move towards the top and it will be uncomfortable on the thighs and chest.
The positioning of the center of gravity, which helps during rotations and jumps, and the saving in energy are the advantages of the seat harness. It is recommended for kiteboarders who have back problems.

The waist harness
It gives more freedom in bending and twisting moves. Yet it makes the abdominal muscles work more than with the seat harness and requires a better balance management during jumps.

The waist harness must stay around your waist and not move up underneath your arms.
Careful ladies, this kind of harness can be uncomfortable and even painful!

Don't neglect the importance of the choice of your harness and don't hesitate to try different ones before selecting yours. If you suffer from back problems, choose the seat harness without giving it a second thought.

The floatation vest

It must correspond to the harness that you use. If you use a waist harness, choose a shorter vest that lets the buckle of the harness pass through.

Select a vest specific to kiteboarding and make sure it doesn't prevent you from making large movements with your shoulders. It should also have a strong fastener that will hold when you body drag.

Equipment

CHOOSING YOUR BOARD

A 1,70 to 2 meter board can be used with both little and a lot of power. It will take less time for beginners to learn how to go upwind, make turns, change direction and jump.
The floatation of a big board brings great comfort when the wind drops and allows going upwind much easier.

A little board of 1,10 to 1,65 meter can only be used with a lot of power in the kite in order to maintain a good edge and go upwind. This requires a good piloting experience and more finesse in the stances on the board.

Custom or production board?

The custom board is hand-made whereas the production board is made according to predetermined moulds. A custom board can be at exactly the size that you want.
If you are not an experienced rider or if you don't know what you want, then the production board is a better choice.

It is only with experience, trying out many different boards, and knowing how they function that you will be able to define your prerequisites for a custom board.

It's nice to talk with other riders, share your knowledge of balance and of direction, your goals and the average number of hours you are going to kiteboard per year before buying a board.

Buying a second hand board

The first thing to check is its general state.

The critical parts are:
The rails: check for holes that will let the water permeate.

The heel stances: if the fiber is soft under the heels, the board is not in good condition and will be less performant.

The inserts: inserts are the holes where the nails of the footstraps are screwed in. Pull firmly on the footstraps to make sure that the nails hold.

Think of your progression! You will need more time to adapt and learn with a little board if you can't go upwind yet.

In any case, trying the board before buying it is the best way to find out if it corresponds to your level of riding and style. Try it with a kite that you are familiar with.

Equipment

Concave: with a scoop flattened in the middle of the board, it gives a good stability, is faster when riding flat on the water and has a good responsiveness in the turns.

Convex: the shape does not make the board stable. The stances on the rails are bad so it is best to avoid it.

The flex: a board can have more or less flex. It influences the scoop of the board, thus its behavior. The upwind abilities are a little lessened by the distortion of the board, but the result of edging can be felt more strongly. Turns can be of a shorter range. Flex gives a feeling of elasticity and absorbs the impacts as well as the energy of the kite. This can give the feeling of having a board that accelerates slower. As for tricks, flex facilitates the rotations that result from edging.

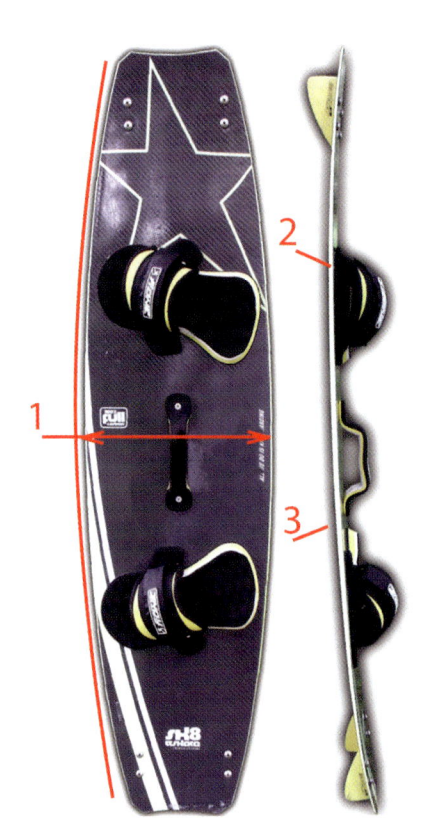

Board characteristics

Scoop ─── Lift

The rocker: it is the curve of the board. The front is defined by the scoop and the back by the lift.

The lift: it is the curve on the back half of the board.
A flatter board has better upwind performance, is faster but isn't easily maneuvered in turns.

A more curved board turns better and is more adapted to wave riding, but performs less well in flat water and when going upwind.

The scoop: it is the curve at the front of the board. This principle can be applied to directional and mutant boards. On a twin tip, the lift and scoop are identical.

The outline (1): it is the maximum width of the board and the shape of the outline.
The outline affects the reaction, the turning speed, the upwind ability, the balance and stability of the board. A board with thin tips is more technical but is less harsh on balance errors. A board with a stiff outline is more stable for upwind riding.

The width: wider boards make it possible to have shorter boards. Regardless of the length, width allows to go upwind and maintain speed without having to manage a lot of power. The width offers better stability when landing aerial tricks, facilitates transitions, and is better in gusty or light wind.

The rail (2): because of its volume and shape, the rail creates the edging of the board in the water. A sharp rail adds performance and helps manage the power, but makes it more difficult to manage with speed because it's more reactive. This kind of rail works well with powerful kites and in flat water.

A round rail with a little volume is more polyvalent and functional. It makes power management easier while riding. But this type of rail is more technical when overpowered.

A few examples of board rails:

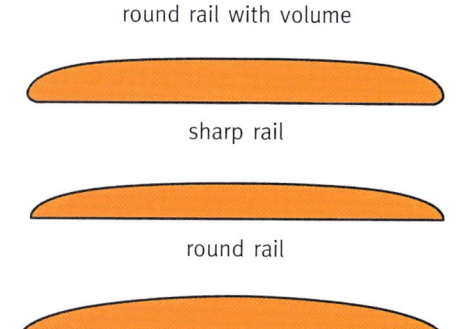

round rail with volume

sharp rail

round rail

The hull (3): it's the part that is in the water. It can be flat, concave or convex, and it can also have channels. Here are the pros and cons of a few hulls.

Flat: a basic hull shape is a little more difficult when kiteboarding flat on the water because it is less stable. This can be easily compensated by fins of a large size. A flat shape works well in turns.

The channels: they alter the scoop and direct the water flow. The board doesn't turn as well, keeping the course is easier and the stability slightly better.

Equipment

THE TWIN TIP OR TT
The TT is the board that has made kiteboarding easier. Just as the directional, the twin tip works for beginners as well as for experienced riders. It's just a matter of choosing the right board size and volume.

THE MUTANT
It's a directional board, with one or more fins at the front that allow riding on the nose when going backwards.
This board works for both surf and free style. There are generally 2 foot straps instead of 3 as on a directional.

THE KITE SKATE
Inspired by wake skate, it is a pure free style board designed for a very specific usage. The only link to the board is a nonskid pad, and the rider makes tricks by making the board spin under his feet (like on a skate board). You should try it, but never without shoes, or you will end up with severely scraped feet.

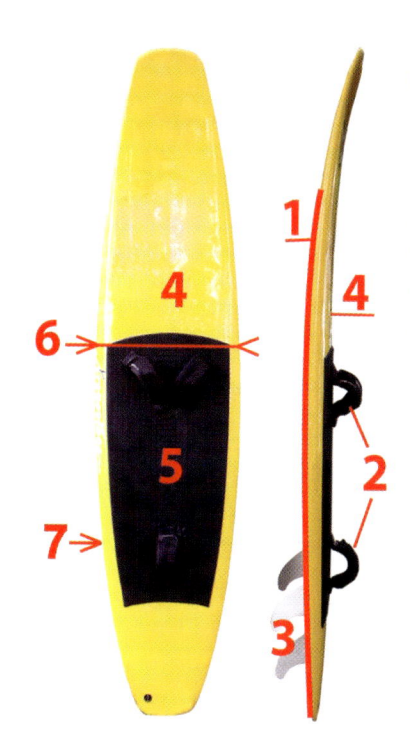

Board terminology
1. *hull*
2. *foot-strap*
3. *fins*
4. *deck*
5. *pads*
6. *outline*
7. *edge*

The different types of boards

THE DIRECTIONAL
It is the perfect board to learn and ride in light wind. Going upwind is easy and does not require much power. It also performs well in waves. Of course, you must learn how to change sides to turn (jibe) but with good advice, you'll see that it is not that hard.

THE WAKEBOARD
Wakeboarding is above all a style. It is ideal for riders who like to handle a lot of power or use 2 line kites. It is also nice for riders who want to do wakeboarding as well as kiteboarding tricks, or just ride and make curves. Apart from the fact that wakeboards have bindings, there are little differences nowadays between a wakeboard and a twin tip.

Equipment

THE BOARD

The shape of the kite boards are in constant evolution to perfect reactivity and performance or meet the needs of new riding styles.

Nowadays, the skill level developed by the shapers makes it possible for anyone to find a board that suits his needs.

It's up to you to choose yours according to your style, weight and practice level.

Equipment

1. leash
2. release system between the leash and the rider
3. releasable center line
4. releasable harness line

Security leash functioning

On a bar set with a fixed leash, the leash must be connected at a distance of half a wingspan on the flying line (see drawing 1).

With a re-riding leash, a stopper (little ball fixed on the same line as the leash) must be fixed at a distance at least equal of a wingspan (A on the drawing page 32) for the safety to work.

2 line bars

2 line safety system

2 line bars must have 3 safety systems:
1. A release on a line or a releasable harness line, also called "active security", that allows to release a line to kill the power of the kite (when the kite is hooked to the harness for instance). You can also use a bar with a releasable harness line.
2. A leash that allows to completely kill the power while staying connected to the kite. The kite can easily be recovered and relaunched. The leash is also used to land alone. Be careful, the length of the leash must correspond to the size of the kite that is used.

   On a bar set with a fixed leash, the leash must be connected to a distance of half a wingspan on the flying line (drawing 1).
   On a bar set with a re-ride system, a stopper (red ball on the drawing 2) must be fixed at a distance at least equal to the kite's wingspan for the safety to work.
3. A leash release, to be used after the bar has been released if the kite continues to pull for an unexpected reason.

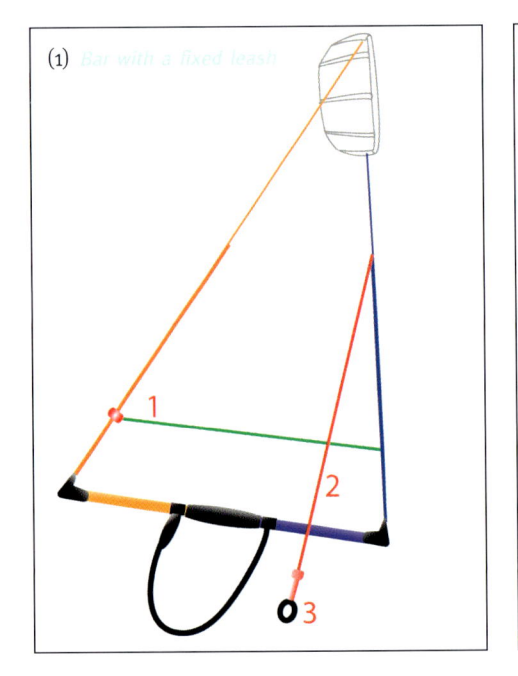

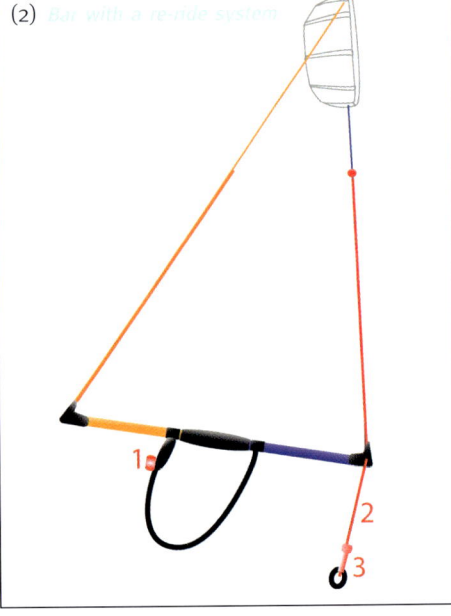

(1) Bar with a fixed leash

(2) Bar with a re-ride system

Adjustable 4 lines
(with a sliding leash system)
This system allows you to immediately adjust the power of the kite, consequently adapting it to the wind changes by moving the bar on the center line. When the bar is held close to you, it increases the power (opposite drawing). When it is held close to the power strap (away from you), it reduces the power (sheeting in and out).

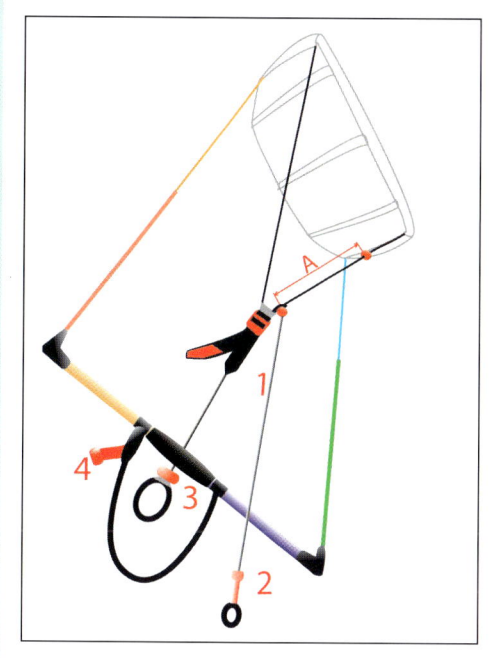

It is the most practical and commonly used bar system.

Make sure you always have a release system on the center line.

Fixed 4 lines
(with a sliding leash system)
This system offers the following alternative: piloting a 4 line kite without being constantly connected to the harness. As on all 4 lines systems, the adjustment is done with the power strap.

The advantages are:
· More responsiveness on low aspect ratio kites
· Possibility to do handle passes (passing the bar from one hand to the next behind the back)
· A bigger wind range compared to a similar kite used with 2 lines.

Using this kind of bar is more technical and physical because the power of the kite is managed by the piloting and edging on the board.

4 lines safety systems
Safety systems are used to kill the power of the kite when necessary.

4 line bars must always have 4 safety components:

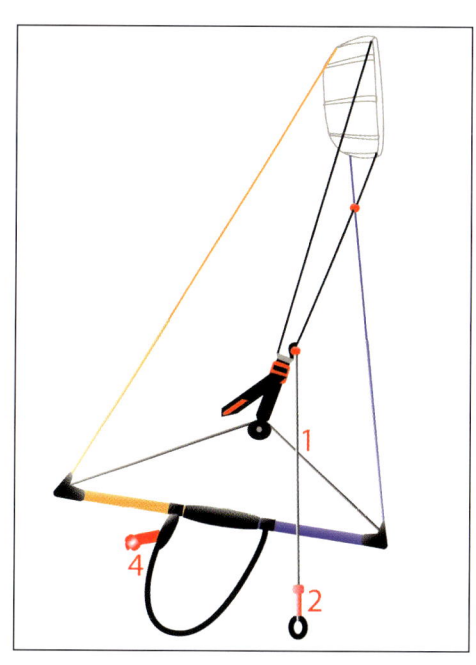

32

Equipment

THE BARS

The bar allows you to manage the power, direction and safety parameters. It must be adapted to the size of your kite. This is normally the case when you purchase a kite and bar of the same brand. The bar must be equipped with a safety system corresponding to the model that you choose.

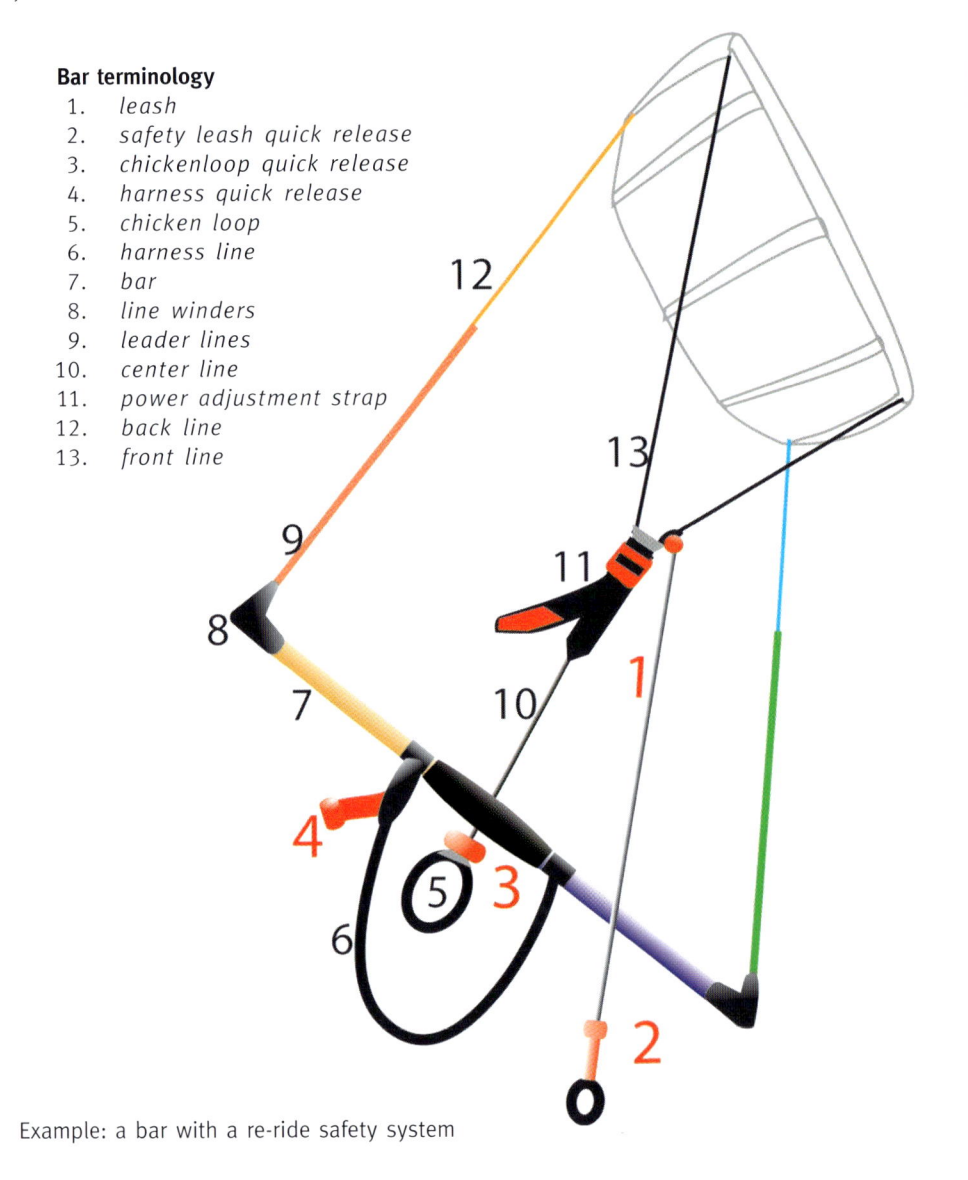

Bar terminology
1. leash
2. safety leash quick release
3. chickenloop quick release
4. harness quick release
5. chicken loop
6. harness line
7. bar
8. line winders
9. leader lines
10. center line
11. power adjustment strap
12. back line
13. front line

Example: a bar with a re-ride safety system

PETER LYNN
KITEBOARDING

WWW.PETERLYNNKITEBOARDING.COM

Equipment

Choosing your kite

You must choose the equipment according to your level. Burning the steps and wanting to look like a professional rider by using the most perfomant kite and the smallest board is useless and might result in putting yourself in a tight spot. With equipment adapted to your level, you will be able to progress and buy more performant equipment later.

Performance or safety?

Ask a qualified instructor to give you advice. Nowadays, nearly all kites have good upwind, power management and jumping performances. But you must take into account that the board and the kite go in pair. If you have less than 40 hours of kiteboarding practice, choose a kite with an average aspect ratio.

Choosing a second hand kite

Here are a few things to check before buying a second hand kite.
Tip: do not look at the kite without sufficiently inflating it and take your time to make sure it stays inflated.

Check list
- **The leading edge** (the biggest bladder): check the seams.
- **The tips:** check the state of the fabric, as launchings and flappings can damage the tips.
- **The trailing edge** (back part of the kite): if the structure of the fabric is not homogenous, (perpendicular fibers), then the fabric is impaired. This does not mean that the kite can not be used, but you should estimate for how long it will hold. Ask the owner if you can slightly pull on the fabric to see if it holds both ways. 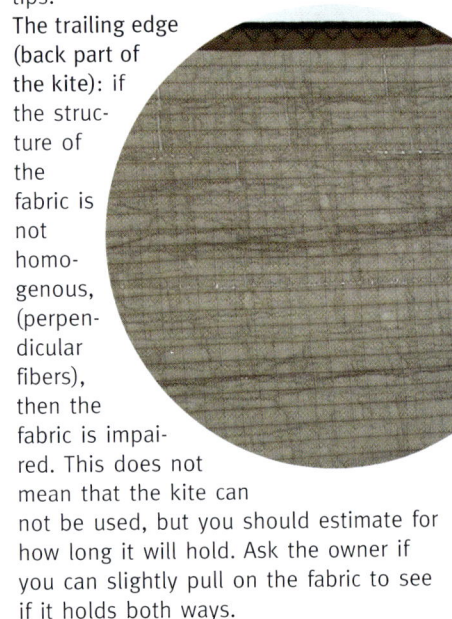
- **The meeting point of the strut and the leading edge:** make sure the leading edge is not impaired by the friction of the strut.

Check the general state and fly the kite to make sure the skin is not loosened or that the kite does not twist.

Test it with your bar or make sure that the lines have the same length before launching the kite.

Maneuvrability

A kite is considered maneuvrable when it follows the movement of the bar without rebound time. The faster the kite responds, the easier it is to jump. On the other hand, mastering aerial jumps is more delicate and requires very precise piloting. To make it easier to fly a kite that is very fast, use a smaller bar. It will slow it down. If on the contrary your kite is too slow, a bigger bar will make it faster.

The aspect ratio

The aspect ratio is the relativity of the wingspan (distance from one tip of the kite to the other, A), and the cord (distance from one side of the bladder to the other, B). A big wingspan and a small cord = high aspect ratio.

The power of the kite is defined by the aspect ratio: the lower the aspect ratio, the more time is needed for the air to cover the surface of the kite, thus the amount of wind turbulence.

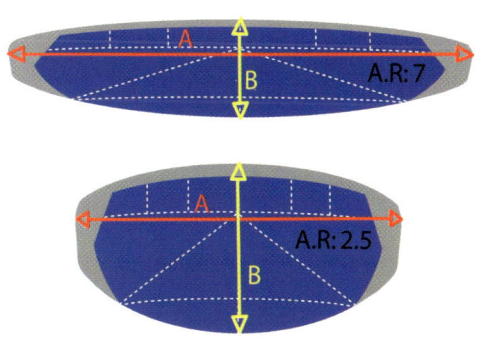

High aspect ratio kites are more performant because their shape creates less wind turbulences. These kites are powerful and reactive to piloting but less stable at neutral and more sentitive to power adjustments. You must have a good piloting level because these kites are harder to relaunch from the water. Low aspect ratio kites are very stable and less reactive to piloting. The lack of power is compensated by using a slightly bigger kite, which makes it more stable when riding and jumping. Easy to learn with, these kites perform well and are easy to relaunch. It's the good choice for beginners who can manage tricks without having a very good piloting level. Most of the recent kites have an aspect ratio well adapted to their surface.

Equipment

CHARACTERISTICS

The surface area of the kites

The surface is one of the criteria that define the power of the kite. Yet all brands do not indicate the actual surface on the kites. Some have a different calculation method and indicate a projected or calculated surface, which roughly corresponds to the surface used. This surface is inferior to the actual surface of the kite.
In order to choose your kite, look at the actual surface. Otherwise, you may think you have bought a 12 m^2 and an 8.5 m^2 kite when in fact you have two kites of the identical size.

The wind range

It is the maximum and minimum wind force in which you can use the kite, according to the weight of the rider and the size of the board.

Brands usually mention the wind range of the kite in their user guide. Check that they are adapted according to your weight and board size. If your board is bigger, you can use the kite with less wind.
Most kites of the same surface have the same wind range. But according to the design, the wind speed, the shape and size of the board, it will be possible to use the same kite in a greater or smaller wind range.
With a big board (180 cm and more), the kite can be used with less wind than with a small board (120 to 160 cm).

A 10 m^2 foil kite has much more power than an inflatable kite of identical size. If you choose a foil kite as alternative kite, check the wind range according to your weight.

Depowering range

It's the possibility to alter the angle between the kite's profile and the wind, which can be more or less big according to the design of each kite. The depowering ability depends on the profile and the shape of the kite and mostly on the position of the connection points between the front and the back lines. A kite that sheets out well has a greater wind range. According to the models, it will require more or less practice in order to be able to evaluate the jumping potentials. It is easier to jump with a kite that does not have too much sheeting out abilities because it does not require sensitive piloting, but it will be much harder to manage the power on the water.

The 4 lines inflatable kite

It is the most popular type of kite. The arc shape gives great aerodynamic stability and spreads the efforts on the entire structure, without using the bridals. The inflatable bladders help maintain the profile and make the wind go in the kite when it falls in the water. This type of kite can be used with a 2 or 4 line bar to manage the power and the adjustments.

The flat inflatable kite

This type of kite lies between the foil and the inflatable arc kite. The shape of the kite is maintained thanks to a bridal on the leading edge. Lines connected to the trailing edge are used to adjust the power and the piloting.

The advantage of these kites is that you can totally reduce their power, which is something the inflatable kites could not do a few years ago. Yet this type of kite is not commonly used.

Two line inflatable kite

These kites are stable and easy to fly and are ideal for beginners. But they require physical strength when used in strong winds because it is impossible to trim the power while kiteboarding.

The number of lines

Kites can be used with 2, 3, 4 and 5 lines according to the models.
Some 2 line kites are also convertible into 4 line kites.
Inflatable 4 line kites are the most commonly used and represent 95% of the market. Foil kites are used with 3 or 4 lines when they have a system to manage the power (the central lines can be joined in one, see picture page 27).

5th line

Some inflatable kites are equipped with a 5th line. It is used to relaunch the kite when it is fixed on the trailing edge and as a safety system when it is fixed on the leading edge.

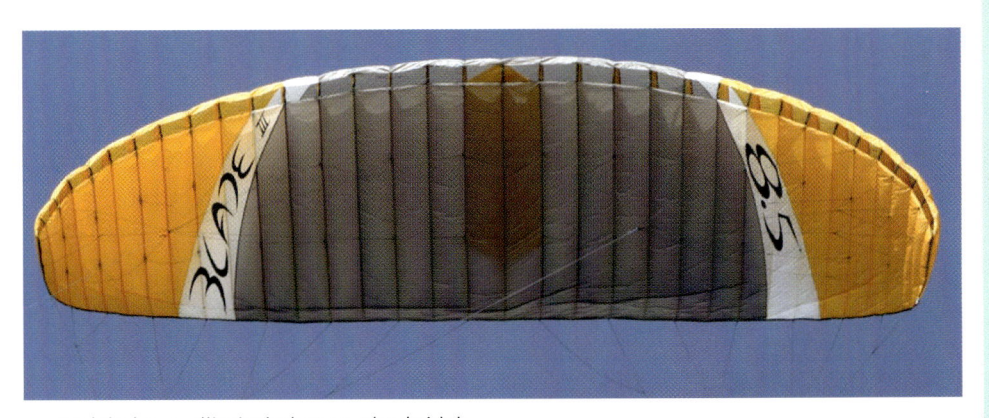

Equipment

models have elliptical shapes; the bridals cross for a better performance during jumps and transitions. Be careful though, this type of kite can not be relaunched from the water. It is not recommended for kiteboarding but it is perfect for snow kite and mountain board.

- Nautical foil kites: they are equipped with vents that keep the air in the kite, making it more stable and easier to relaunch from the water. The nautical foil kites can also be set at different angles of attack, meaning that the angle of the kite can be changed to manage the power according to the wind.

- The arc kites: they look like inflatable semi elliptical kites and work with the same principle. They are connected with 4 lines, 2 for the power and 2 for piloting and power management. The advantage is the simplicity of preparing the equipment. Moreover, bridals are unnecessary with the arc shape.

Foil kites are most often used in areas where the wind is light. The flat foil kites are harder to control when the wind is unstable, which is one of the reasons why a lot of kiteboarders use inflatable or arc kites. Nevertheless, innovations in equipment have rendered the performance of various kites almost equal.

THE KITES

Kites come in different shapes and colors, so there is certainly a kite for you. But how can we tell the difference from one to the next?

Kite terminology

Whether for foil or inflatable kites, the same terminology is used.
1. *top skin (extrados)*
2. *lower skin (intrados)*
3. *leading edge*
4. *trailing edge*
5. *struts*
6. *tips*
7. *back pig tail knots*
8. *front pig tail knots*
9. *bridals*

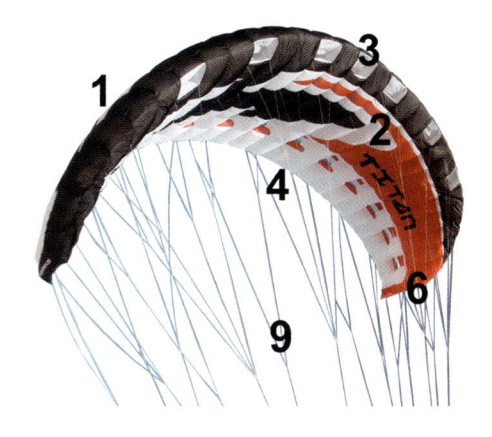

The different types of kites

Being familiar with the different types of kites is useful to understand the way they function and how to select your equipment. A general description will help you choose the best one for you.

Single skin kites

The most well know single skin kite is the «NASA wing». A big delta kite is also a single skin kite. It is the oldest type of kite and even though it is powerful, its performance is not really adapted to kiteboarding because it can't be relaunched from the water and it is very difficult to go upwind. Even though not advised for kiteboarding practice, single skin kites can be piloted with 2 or 4 lines, for power management.

Foil kites

These kites use the twin skin technology. Air intake vents on the leading edge allow the kites to inflate and maintain an airplane profile.

There are different types of foil kites:
· Classic foil kites: the shape of the kite is maintained thanks to bridals that are spread on the entire surface of the kite. The first foil kites had a rectangular shape and were not very performant. More recent

The kites
Characteristics
The bars
The board
Choosing your board
The rider's equipment

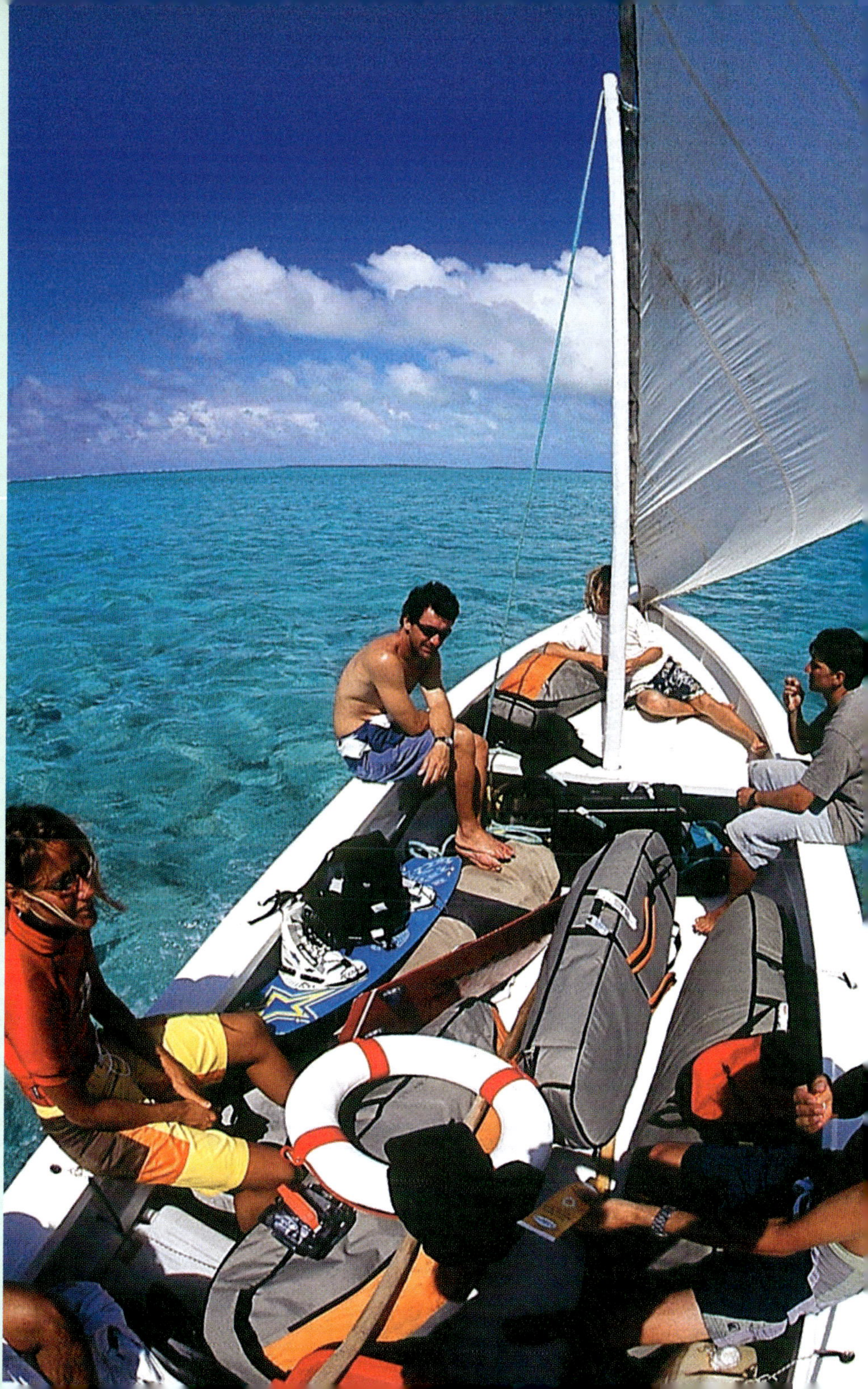

Safety

over them, be tempted to take the bar in his hands, unaware of the consequences, or the kite might fly off and create hazards.

Don't jump when you are close to the shore or close to an obstacle.

FOR THOSE WHO ARE WATCHING

People usually don't hesitate to come get a closer look at kiteboarding. Share these few rules with them:
Don't come between the rider and the kite (risks with the lines).

If you ask a passer by to help you land your kite, take time to explain what he must do. He must not move but wait until you bring the kite close to him, then he must grab it by the main bladder (leading edge) and hold it firmly until you have recovered it. To help your assistant hold the kite, release the tension from the lines by walking towards the kite as soon as he has grabbed it.

HELMET OR NO HELMET?

If you have been lucky to never have the board land on your head or if you never fell on the ground, then you probably think that the helmet is for the inexperienced. Some people even think that it is not stylish.
Since most accidents result in injuries to the head, it's always best to wear a helmet.

A helmet will protect you:
- if you use a board leash (even if it is long or with a winding system)
- when you try new tricks
- when you use new equipment
- when you kiteboard on a very crowded spot.

If you choose not to wear a helmet, you must assume responsibilities, knowing what the consequences could be.

Whether you wear a helmet or not, you must always stay away from obstacles and from the shore. And most importantly, you must know how to body drag upwind to recover your board because if you do not wear a helmet, it means you do not use a board leash.

The helmet can never be considered as an unnecessary protection because it also protects you from other riders.

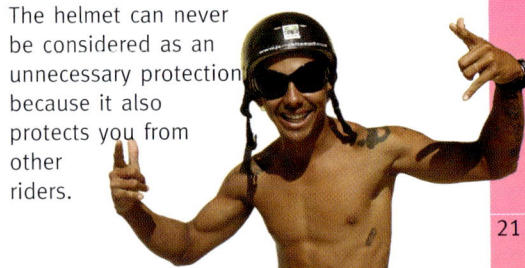

21

Kiteboarding is a leisure sport and in order for it to remain a pleasure, safety must be respected. Either on land or in the water, our safety and the safety of other riders and beach users depend on all of us.

SAFETY ADVICE

Check your equipment before each session and most importantly, check that the lines are connected properly before launching your kite.

Always use a kite leash, connect it before launching and keep it connected until landing. Letting go of your kite without a leash may result in loosing your equipment, or create an accident if your lines get tangled in another kite or hit a passer-by.

Wear a helmet, especially if you are using a board leash (connect it right before going in the water) and a floatation or protection vest. Go in the water as soon as you have launched your kite and don't put it at the top of the wind window until you are close to the water or sure that the wind is not too strong or unstable.

Never grab two lines at the same time. The kite lines could injure your fingers if they regain tension. On the other hand, if the wind is not too strong, you can grab a line to walk to your kite and recover it.

Don't go away from the shore at a further distance than the one you can swim back from with your equipment.

Disconnect the lines of your kite when you leave it on the ground. Someone could trip

Safety

Safety advice
For those who are watching
Helmet or no helmet?

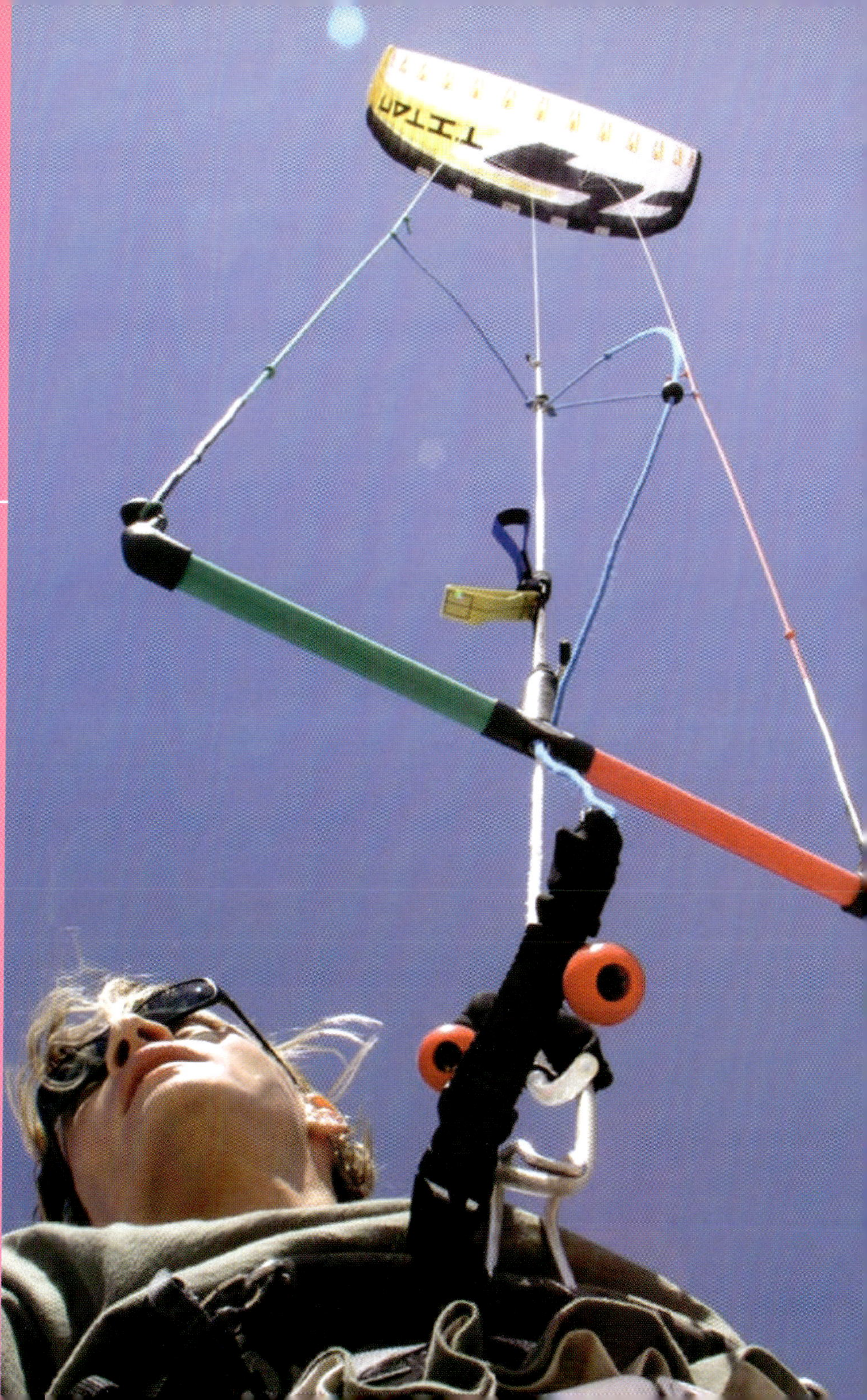

Introduction

someone is observing you and will help you whenever necessary.

If you doubt your ability to ride on your own, choose this kind of service. You have everything to gain from it: safety, easiness and a friendly environment.

Progression

Progression is a matter of time, determination, and sometimes equipment. You will find an answer to most questions in this book. Be wary of the advice of riders that "know it all", because advanced riders will not necessarily give you the advice required at your level.

A good piece of advice is the one that makes you progress immediately and allows you to auto evaluate yourself.

Do not hesitate to return to a school to perfect your kiteboarding skills and learn how to perform tricks.

KITEBOARDING TERMS

Just as every other sport, kiteboarding has its own language and vocabulary.

Technical terms refer to the equipment, riding, and to different tricks and jumps. To make the reading easier, technical terms are transcribed in a common language and are accompanied by drawings at the beginning of each chapter. A glossary of the technical terms is available at the end of the book.

WARNING

A well informed kiteboarder is worth two kiteboarders!
Having adequate knowledge will result in safer riding and ultimately more fun. Most accidents occur because the wind and weather are not properly analysed and because the safety distances between the riders and the obstacles are not respected. The biggest dangers are carelessness and ignorance that regroup the following behavior patterns: riding in very turbulent wind, riding upwind to obstacles, buildings, cliffs, excelling oneself to impress others, not observing the sky and the clouds, not caring about the weather forecast, not caring about other riders, not respecting the priority rules, never being afraid, not setting the equipment properly, not having safety gear or not making sure it functions in live situations.

To practice with confidence and in a safe manner, we must first observe the obstacles that create wind turbulences, check the weather forecast, and avoid kiteboarding with onshore or offshore wind.

Most accidents can be avoided by common sense, comprehension and application of the knowledge developed in this book, and by observing what is going on around you.

As for the safety systems, learn their functioning by heart. You must be able to trigger the safety system without having to think. Repeat the movement before each ride and check that the safety system is at hands' reach and that is works before using your kite for the first time.

DISCOVER, PRACTICE

Kiteboarding is an easy sport, as easy as driving a car or a little boat, but it can be just as dangerous if we don't learn how to practice in a school.
And even though it is simple, the lack of knowledge as far as safety and priority rules are concerned can turn an adventure into a problem or even an accident, for you and for other kiteboarders.

Learning in a school with a qualified instructor will minimize the risks as much as possible. From the start, you will learn different safety procedures and how to respond thanks to adapted practical exercises so that whatever the conditions you meet, you will become an independent rider quicker.

The first independent sessions

In order to become an independent kiteboarder, you must be able to evaluate the risks and know how to avoid them. But most importantly, you must know your limits! Practice in a club, either with a friend or an assistant who will be able to help you. Don't hesitate to walk a little further away from the other beach users, and always prefer a smaller kite size when you are not sure which size to choose.

Supervised practice

Kiteboarding schools or clubs offer a supervised practice service. This ensures that

Introduction

Kiteboarding's image is extreme, but it is a sport that can be practiced and enjoyed by many. The efforts in research and development should allow more people to enjoy it in the near future. Let's hope that the designers will not only work on performance but on accessibility and simplicity as well.

THE STORY

The invention of kites is credited to two Chinese men at the end of the 5th century and beginning of the 4th BC. Since then, kites have been used for various purposes: in 1232, the Chinese used them to send messages to the prisoners behind the Mongolian lines, motivating them to start riots and escape.

Considered as religious relics in Peru, huge kites are still built and require many dozens of men to make them fly. They can also be used as fishing tools when used with a second line fixed with a hook. In western culture, they are used for leisure purposes...

What if we could sail with a kite? The history of kiteboarding started in the 70s.
At that time, a few people were seen as they were pulled on water skis by kites. In 1977, Gilbertus Panhuise used a windsurfing board and obtained a patent for the concept.
During the 80s, Andreas Kuhn was on TV with a wakeboard, pulled by a 25m^2 paraglide.

In 1984, Dominique and Bruno Legaignoux registered the patent for water relaunchable inflatable kites. These kites were immediately tested with windsurfing boards and water skis.
At the end of the 80s, Cory Roeseler developed the "Kiteski" by using motorcycle breaks' spare parts in order to build a bar with a winding system, making it possible to launch a delta wing from the water. He obtained a patent in 1992.

In 1995, Laird Hamilton and Manu Bertin drew the attention of the media as they started kiteboarding using Wipika sails and windsurfing boards. From this point onwards, the development of the sport took yet another turn. In 1997, F-One was the first brand to market the production of kiteboarding boards.

In September 1998, the first competition took place in Maui and was won by Flash Austin. 1998 was also the year when windsurfing legend Robby Naish started kiteboarding.
Today, kiteboarding has reached worldwide dimensions.

Many brands sell equipment, competitions are held and organizations such as the IKO have been founded in order to ensure the safe growth and promotion of the sport at an international level.

Introduction

KITEBOARD

Here we go! The only thing that we can hear when kiteboarding is the wind in the lines and the water under our board! A big smile on his face, eyes wide open, a beginner has just made his first ride! Those who have passed this step know what it feels like. They also know that it's only the beginning!

Kiteboarding is a manifold activity, a bit like music: with the same instrument, we can play all sorts of styles. A kite, the size of which varies from 3 to 22 m^2, conveys the power of the wind to the kiteboarder, who rides on a 0,90 to 2,30 meter board.

WELCOME NOTE

Kiteboarding is easy: all you need to do to open the gate to endless sensations is to fly the kite and stand on the board! This is true, but under the condition that you've learnt with professionals who have given you the necessary knowledge to become an independent rider. Knowing how to ride on a board with a kite is only part of the sport. Just as for paragliding or sailing, knowledge of the weather and safety procedures is mandatory. You can not learn how to kiteboard alone by reading this book. It does not replace the personalized advice and the corrections that a qualified instructor will give you during your training. This book is a source of general, technical and practical information aimed at a larger audience.
Using this book in order to practice kiteboarding is at the sole responsibility of the reader!

1 Introduction

Welcome note
Kiteboard
The story
Discover, Practice
Kiteboarding terms

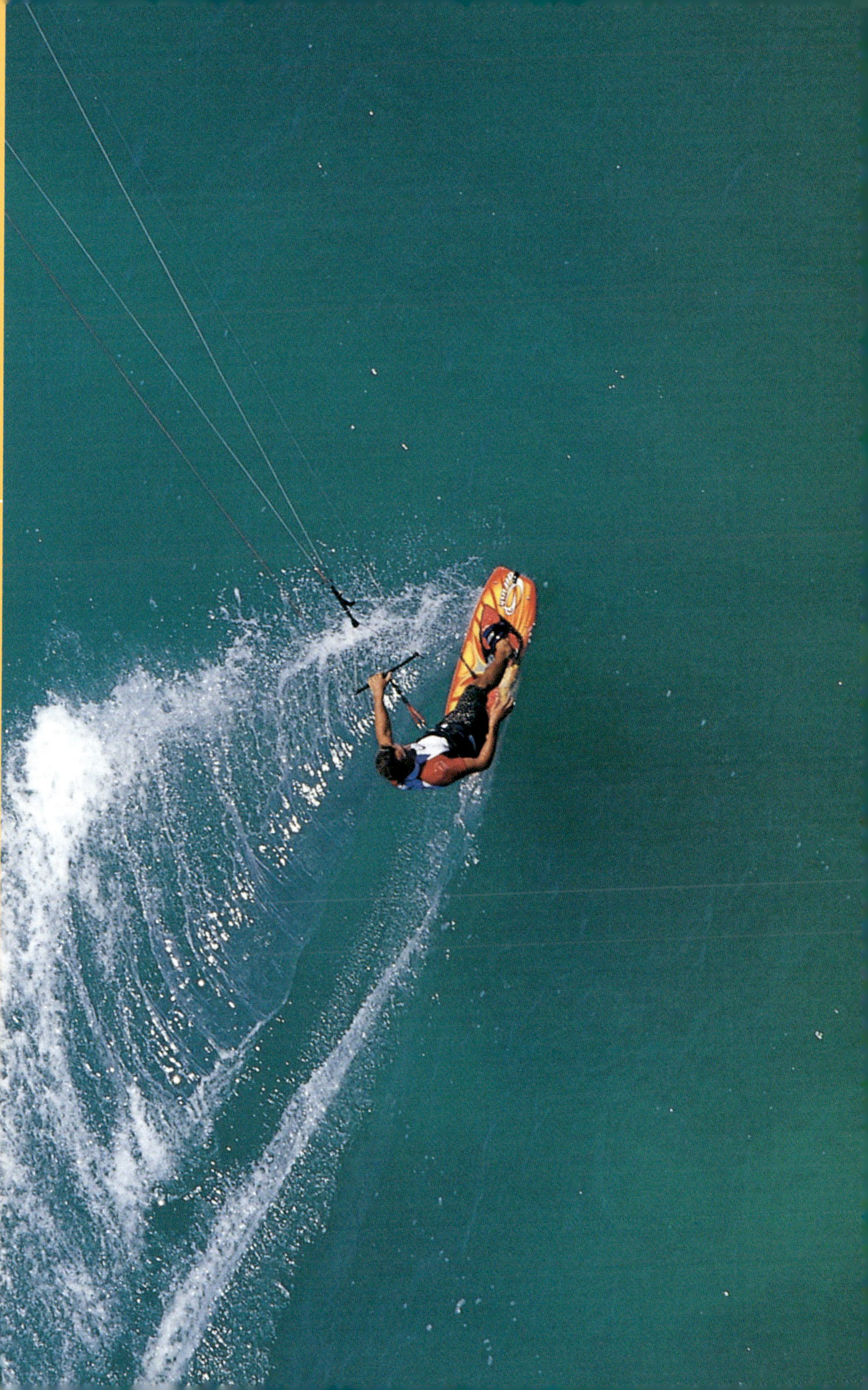

CONTENTS

IMPROVEMENT

Change of direction with a twin tip	84
Body dragging upwind	84
The jibe	85
Riding toe side	86
Surfing a wave	86
The first jump	87
Improving your jump	89
The tricks	90
Blind or backwards	90
The jump with a transition	91
The long jump	91
The high jump	91
The back loop	92
The grabs	94
Backwards 360° with change of direction	95
360° front rotation	95
Front loop	95
Jumping head upside down (inverted)	95
The dead man	98
The tantrum	98
No foot or board off	98
Evolution	99

FROM WIND TO TRACTION

The length of the lines	102
Aerodynamics	102
Why can we jump?	108

METEOROLOGY

The tides	112
Discover the weather	114

OTHER TRACTION SPORTS

The mountain board	120
Snow kite	120
Buggy	121

PRACTICAL TOOLS

The knots	124
Intl. kiteboarding signs	125
Kiteboarder's glossary	126

TABLE OF

INTRODUCTION
Welcome note	12
Kiteboard	13
The story	14
Discover, Practice	16
Kiteboarding terms	17

SAFETY
Safety advice	20
For those who are watching	21
Helmet or no helmet?	21

EQUIPMENT
The kites	24
Characteristics	27
The bars	31
The board	34
Choosing your board	40
The rider's equipment	42

PRACTICE
Directions	46
Navigation terminology	46
The wind window	48
The compass rose	49
Getting ready	50
Rigging and launching	54
Landing the kite	59
Launching the kite from the water	60
The water start	62
The stance	68
Balance	69
Slowing down and stopping	70
Managing the power	72
Going upwind	74
Troubles and remedies	76
Priority rules	80
Equipment tips	81

Preface

PREFACE

The purpose of this book is not to praise kiteboarding, but gather technical, practical and even historical information related to the sport.

Either to discover or perfect your skills, Kiteboarding Vision will help you become familiar with the world of kiteboarding and expand your knowledge in essential fields. You will learn how to react in different situations and you will be guided throughout your progress.

I hope you will enjoy reading this book and that it will salt your future kiteboarding sessions. Don't keep your feet too much on the ground!

Eric Beaudonnat

Kiteboarding Vision

© Copyrigth 2004 Eric Beaudonnat, IKO. All rights reserved.
No part of this publication may be reproduced, copied, transmitted, in any form or by any means, without the author's prior written authorization.

Artwork: Armando Domenech
Cover picture: Airush, rider Félix Pivec
Printed in April 2004
ISBN 99934-999-0-0

The essential to discover,
learn and improve kiteboarding